WILLIAM WHITEWAY
OF DORCHESTER

His Diary 1618 to 1635

DORSET RECORD SOCIETY

VOLUME 12

Published 1991 Dorset Record Society
Dorset County Museum, Dorchester, Dorset

Designed by Laurence Keen
Typeset in Linotronic Baskerville by Character Graphics, Taunton, Somerset
and printed by Henry Ling Ltd., The Dorset Press, Dorchester
on Ganton Antique Wove 80gsm vol 17.5.
Cover Lugo Grandee 216gsm.

British Library Cataloguing in Publication Data
Whiteway, William 1599-1635
William Whiteway of Dorchester: his diary, 1618-1635.
1. Dorset (England), history, 1603-1649
I. Title II. Dorset Record Society
942.331061

ISBN 0-900339-11-X

Cover illustration: Dorchester, from J. Speed's Map of Dorset 1610

The Society is grateful to the
Somerset & Dorset Family History Society
and to the Friends of Dorset's Archives
for contributions towards this publication.

CONTENTS

ACKNOWLEDGEMENTS

Selections from the journal of William Whiteway and from his commonplace book were published by the Revd. W. Miles Barnes in 1892 and 1895 in the *Proceedings of the Dorset Natural History and Antiquarian Field Club*, Vol. 13, pp. 57-81, and Vol. 16, pp. 59-74, and a transcript of the journal was included in the doctoral thesis lodged in the library of Yale University by Thomas D. Murphy in 1939. But though the importance of the journal has been known to scholars for many years, hitherto no printed text has been available. The full text of Whiteway's journal (BL Egerton 784) is published now by permission of the Trustees of the British Library. It has also been possible, by courtesy of the Yale University Librarian, to include selections from the biographical notes in Murphy's thesis as an appendix.

The Society owes a debt of gratitude to all who have shared in the present volume: to Mr Brian Bates, who initiated the project by his enthusiasm, transcribing the journal afresh and generously allowing the Society the use of his microfilm; to Miss Sarah Bridges, who has spent many hours patiently and skilfully sorting out the tangles of a very difficult text; to Miss Margaret Holmes, Mr George Clarke and Mr Hugh Jaques, who, in various ways, have made essential contributions to the explanatory material in the book; and to Mr Laurence Keen, who has undertaken the task of seeing the volume through the press. Finally, the Society wishes to record its thanks to Professor David Underdown of Yale University for his masterly introduction.

[6]

NOTE ON THE TEXT

The diary is a leather-bound volume measuring 140 x 80 mm and containing 121 parchment folios. There are 222 pages of diary entries, though these are numbered to 224 since pages 11 and 12 are omitted. Before the diary entries proper and on the first few pages, there are various notes and rough jottings, all of which have been transcribed in Appendix 1. Here too will be found an inventory of plate and other notes written on the volume's final pages. A coat of arms, not connected with the Whiteway family though presumably drawn by the diarist, appears at the beginning of the volume.

The printed transcript reflects the original text as closely as possible, but inconsistencies in the diarist's style make some standardisation necessary, particularly for dates and lists. Sometimes the diarist centres the date above an entry; at other times he uses it to start a paragraph and then runs straight on. Nor is he consistent in the way he records the dates themselves, but includes or omits day, month or year of an entry, and varies their order indiscriminately. Dates therefore have been standardised to include the day and the month for each entry, and the year has been added only for the first entry of a new year, both new and old style – that is, after 1 January and 25 March. There is also considerable variation in the way the diarist records lists of recently married or dead people, and of candidates elected to borough and parliamentary office. These too have been laid out in a standardised way.

All spelling has been retained as in the original, and so has the diarist's random use of upper and lower case letters, except at the start of a new sentence, where modern practice has been adopted. But it must be added that it is often difficult to decide if he is using a capital letter or not. His liberal use of punctuation has been reproduced unless it is misleading.

[7]

Throughout the diary Whiteway employs many standard abbreviations for titles, christian names, places and sums. These have been silently expanded, except for abbreviations such as Exon. and Oxon. found in common usage today. He also uses a mixture of arabic and roman numerals in accounts of men slain, sums spent etc.; all have been transcribed in arabic. His various quotations in Latin, Greek and Italian have been reproduced in the original language, followed by suggested English translations in italics.

In general, any editiorial additions or deduced readings are indicated by square brackets.

INTRODUCTION

David Underdown

HISTORIANS have sometimes depicted seventeenth-century Englishmen as an incurably parochial lot. Tucked away in their cottages and manor houses or little country towns, we have been told, they had little interest in or knowledge of the world beyond their parish boundaries.[1] That this was not always the case is evident from the diary of William Whiteway of Dorchester: Whiteway shows an absorbing interest in the great events that were shaking both England and the whole continent of Europe between 1618, when he first started to record them, and his untimely death in 1635. His diary provides a window into the mental world of a prosperous and well educated provincial townsman. Far from being merely localist, it illustrates the interaction between the various circles of its author's existence: the circles of family and kin; of town and region; of country and kingdom; and of the wider world beyond its shores. All these circles of existence were linked within a framework of Christian beliefs, about God and the individual's role in the eternal struggle between good and evil in which the diarist was conscious that he had a crucial part to play.

The Whiteways were not, of course, an ordinary Dorchester family. Although relative newcomers to the town (the diarist's father, William the elder, had settled there only in 1600, the year after the diarist was born),[2] they were, by Dorchester standards, wealthy and well-connected. The elder Whiteway was a member of the town government at least by 1610, and moved up rapidly through the local hierarchies of wealth and office; the family's status was confirmed in 1620 by the diarist's marriage to Elinor, daughter of another prominent figure in Dorchester's governing circle, John Parkins. And William's brother John was soon to marry the niece of the town's formidable rector, John White.[3]

[9]

That William Whiteway's life was strongly rooted in family and kin is evident in the repeated notices of the births, marriages, and deaths of cousins, aunts, uncles, brothers- and sisters-in-law which appear in such profusion both in the diary and in the 'Private Chronology' in his commonplace book.[4] Like all English diarists before Samuel Pepys, Whiteway is reticent about his personal feelings. Early in the diary there is a youthful love-poem (there may have been others, later crossed out), but he tells us nothing about his courtship of Elinor, about the extent to which it was an arranged marriage (there certainly were some careful financial arrangements), and almost nothing about the wedding, apart from the inscription on the ring and the fact that 'the greatest part of the Towne attended" [14 June 1620].[5] Nor does he reveal his feelings about the births and sadly recurrent early deaths – of six out of seven born between 1621 and 1633 – of his and Elinor's children. Unlike his more plebeian contemporary, the Londoner Nehemiah Wallington, who agonized over similar tragedies, he never records anything more heartfelt that the conventional 'God took her unto his mercy'.[6] He was away on a sightseeing trip to London when one child died, though it may be that her illness had hastened his return [28 Oct. 1634]. But while emotional intensity is absent, in his obsessive recording of the comings and goings of kinsfolk, and of their life-cycle events, Whiteway shows that to a very large degree his sense of identity was bound up with that of his family.

Besides being a Whiteway, William was also a Dorchester man. As with family matters, many of the diary's entries on town affairs simply provide a neutral record of births, marriages and deaths, of appointments to civic office, or of the movements of the clergy of the town's three parishes. But he also gives us some inklings of the sort of events that must have been major topics of conversation in the Dorchester of the 1620s and early 1630s. We hear of the occasional public calamities: the big fire of January 1623 (there had been an even bigger one in August 1613 when William was still at the Grammar School), the 1624 smallpox epidemic, the 1630 dearth. There are a few sensational crimes and accidents, most of which would have had their counterparts in any small town of the period. But during Whiteway's lifetime, for reasons to be explained later, Dorchester was going through a period of remarkable civic improvement. He records many of the visible signs of this process: the rebuilding of the Grammar School, the foundation of the new Trinity (elementary) school; the establishment of a municipal brewery to help finance the poor relief system; the new gaol; the enlargement of All Saints church. In 1629 Dorchester got a new charter making it for the first time a mayoral town (until then its government had been headed by two Bailiffs) and giving new powers to the corporation – a development that led to the only outbreak of serious internal strife that Whiteway narrates, the conflict between the Capital Burgesses and the members of the Company of Freemen in the autumn of 1631 [6 Oct. 1629; 16 Sept. and 5 Dec. 1631].

Whiteway was proud of his town, and of his and his father's roles in it through their numerous civic offices. In 1625 he compiled a detailed account of Dorchester's charitable institutions – the almshouses, the Hospital (actually a workhouse for poor children), the Free School, the various gifts and bequests to the town's poor, the monies collected in the three churches for charitable purposes – as well as lists of town properties and officeholders.[7] These things were important and ought to be painstakingly recorded. But the town of Dorchester was not the limit of William's mental horizon. Although a corporate borough with its own courts and magistrates, Dorchester was also within the county of Dorset, which formed the next in the series of concentric circles of existence that made up Whiteway's world.

As a record of county events the diary is naturally far less complete than it is for the town. Still, it indicates that its author took a keen interest in the lives and deaths of the leading gentry of his neighbourhood. He picks up occasional gossip about melodramatic incidents like Clement Walker's stabbing his wife at the dinner table, or the execution of the Earl of Castlehaven for a series of unnatural sex crimes that took place at his mansion at Fonthill, just over the Wiltshire border. The county's afflictions are also described: fires at Poole and Blandford, for example, and the outbreaks of plague that led to the cancellation of Woodbury Hill Fair for three successive years. Sessions of the Assizes, major events in any county town, are regularly noted, as are ecclesiastical visitations by the Bishop of Bristol or the local Archdeacon. Apart from High Sheriffs and the MPs for the county and its various boroughs, Whiteway gives only sporadic information about county officeholders. When he notes the appointment or dismissal of JPs it is sometimes because political considerations were involved [27 July 1626;

[11]

28 Nov. 1628]. He takes rather more interest in the affairs of the county militia, doubtless because he was himself an officer.

Whiteway's preoccupation with the affairs of his town and county was accompanied by an intense curiosity about the world beyond their boundaries. Many of his entries illustrate the growing impact of national government on the locality, and often relate to issues that were beginning to cause serious divisions in the kingdom. He was a loyal subject who routinely recorded royal occasions, duly noting that a new star appeared after the birth of the prince, the future King Charles II, on 29 May 1630; a conforming member of the Church of England, whose discipline was 'our discipline' [Feb. 1633/4]; and a patriotic Englishman who expectantly followed the progress of English military and naval expeditions to Cadiz, the Isle de Rhé, and La Rochelle, dutifully noting their infrequent successes and lamenting the more numerous occasions when they ingloriously returned without accomplishing anything. There is nothing in his diary to suggest that Whiteway, even as late as 1635, sensed the possibility that within a very few years Englishmen would be fighting each other in a bitter civil war over the governance of church and state. But that both Whiteway and some of his contemporaries were dissatisfied with many aspects of that governance the diary makes abundantly clear.

Whiteway is, to be sure, almost as reticent about his politics as he is about his personal life. As with local affairs, many of his entries dealing with national government are politically neutral: news about noblemen and courtiers, the creation of peers, the appointment of judges and officers of state. Highly controversial events are often recorded without a flicker of comment. Whiteway obviously had little time for the King's great minister, the Duke of Buckingham, yet he shows no sign of rejoicing at the news of the Duke's assassination in August 1628, simply reporting it and adding only the alleged justification spoken by the assassin. The savage punishment inflicted by Star Chamber on the Somerset lawyer William Prynne, for alleged aspersions on the Queen in his notorious attack on stage plays, is noted with similar discretion, Whiteway's sympathies appearing only in the statement that Prynne 'endured his mutilation with much courage' [7 May 1634]. For the most part Whiteway (wisely, for these were dangerous times) keeps his opinions to himself.

It is largely in his choice of the events to be recorded that Whiteway's political stance is revealed. He did not fill his diary with admiring accounts of events at Court, glowing tributes to Archbishop Laud's ceremonial innovations, or reflections that would indicate a general sense of harmony in the kingdom. He filled it, to a quite striking degree, with references to contentious events that demonstrated the existence of serious national divisions. There is something highly symbolic in the fact that the diary begins, after the routine list of local officeholders, with the comet of 1618 (which, though Whiteway does not explicitly say so, to many people seemed to presage great disturbances in the world), and then continues with the execution of Sir Walter Ralegh, the last great representative of Elizabethan hostility to Catholic Spain, a policy on which the pacific James I had ostentatiously turned his back.

The diary often dwells on matters that reveal the restiveness of local opinion in the face of the intrusive policies of the central government. Thus, with the coming of war with Spain (James was reluctantly pushed into it in 1624), and later France, there are many references to the conscription and billeting of troops in Dorset. The soldiers, unpaid, mutinous and disorderly, were the cause of much resentment in the neighbourhood. Some of them were rounded up and condemned to death after a series of burglaries, but as Whiteway notes, they were promptly pardoned by the crown [17 Jan. 1626/7]. When Parliament assembled in 1628, Sir Walter Erle, MP for Dorset, vigorously expressed the county's sense of outrage. The soldiers, he declared, 'rob men on the highway, ravish women, breaking houses in the night and enforcing men to ransom themselves, killing men that have assisted constables that have come to keep the peace'.[8] Grievances about billeting were to figure prominently in the debates over the Petition of Right, the great statement of the subject's liberties that the House of Commons drew up later in the session. It is not surprising to find Whiteway's fellow-townsmen refusing to billet soldiers they thought they had at last got rid of in April 1628.[9]

The crown's financial exactions were another source of grievance. It is of course true that people in all times and places have always disliked taxation, and attempts to evade it do not necessarily indicate any fundamental alienation from the regime in power. It was the form rather than the fact of early Stuart taxation that caused the trouble. As the 1620s wore on there were increasing signs that Charles I was determined to exact it even when it was denied him by Parliament, from time immemorial the accepted institution to legitimize taxes over and above the crown's ordinary, permanent revenues. Taxes levied in 'a parliamentary way' caused no serious resentment: Whiteway does not mention any when he notes Dorchester's assessment for the 1624 parliamentary subsidy. It was only when Charles I repeatedly attempted to by-pass Parliament altogether that Whiteway began to show as much interest in the resistance to taxation as he did in the taxation itself. When Charles tried to borrow £100,000 from the City of London, he could get less than a quarter of that amount, and from the aldermen only. When the King appealed to his subjects for a 'Benevolence' or 'Free Gift', all that Whiteway tells us about the response is that there was 'very little given', and that mainly by the Catholics [8 Aug. 1626]. Whether or not this was true is beside the point: the significant thing is that this is how Whiteway records the information.

A similar emphasis is also present in his discussions of the much more contentious matter of the Forced Loan of 1626-27.[10] He notes that the 'greatest part' of the peers eventually paid what was asked of them, and that there were only four refusers, albeit prominent ones, in the entire county of Dorset. But he dwells far more on the widespread reluctance to pay that was evident in some other parts of the country [Nov. 1626; Jan. 1626/7; Apr. 1627]. If Whiteway were our only source, all we should know about the collection of Tunnage and Poundage without parliamentary consent after 1628 is that there was a 'general refusal' by merchants to pay it, and that those who caved in under pressure were 'much hated' by their neighbours, not that the levy was in fact generally paid [19 May 1629]. Of the King's other non-parliamentary revenue expedients, the first time Whiteway mentions composition for knighthood it is only with the addition that 'it raised little money for most men made excuses' [15 Sept. 1630; but cf. 20 Apr. 1631]. Whiteway died before the critical stages of the campaign to levy the best-known and most productive of Charles I's exactions, Ship Money, but he had some details of the initial response, again noting widespread evasion in London and elsewhere, assessment disputes in Dorset, and the news that the rate was paid in Dorchester 'with much grudging' [28 Nov. 1634; 1 Jan. 1634/5].

This striking interest in manifestations of resistance to taxation without consent of Parliament does not mean that Whiteway was part of, or was even conscious of, any organized 'opposition' to the

[14]

crown.[11] He had good sources of information about parliamentary developments. His father-in-law, John Parkins, was one of the MPs of Dorchester in 1621, his own father in 1624 and 1625, and William himself was elected during the latter part of the 1626 Parliament, after the death of Michael Humphreys, though there is no evidence that he actually attended. So he can provide reasonably accurate (though far from complete) summaries of proceedings in all these parliaments, whereas his accounts of the turbulent sessions of 1628 and 1629, when neither he nor any of his close relations were in the Commons, are the sketchiest of the lot.

Whiteway's impressions of these parliaments are not very different from those which can be derived from other sources. There was some friction in 1621, over the Commons' attempts to insist on harsher treatment of Catholic recusants and to infringe on the King's foreign policy prerogatives, and the session was followed by the imprisonment of two of the most vocal members, Sir Edward Coke and Sir Robert Phelips. But 1624 was a model of harmony, James I having surrendered to the anti-Spanish policies pressed on him by his son and the Duke of Buckingham, and supported by a majority of the Commons. Signs of serious conflict appear, in Whiteway as in other sources, only after Charles I's accession. The Parliament of 1625 was dissolved, he tells us, 'with great dislike on both sides' – a significant choice of language, for according to the prevailing theory of consensus, there could be no such thing as political 'sides' in seventeenth-century England [Aug. 1625]. The 1626 Parliament promptly embarked on a vigorous campaign to impeach the King's powerful chief minister, Buckingham, and was frustrated only by a timely dissolution. Whiteway's dislike of Buckingham is very clear. His commonplace book contains derogatory verses and anecdotes about the Duke,[12] while the diary reports several riotous attacks on him by mutinous sailors, which effectively emphasize the affront to the great man's dignity. After Buckingham's military disgrace in the Isle de Rhé the diarist acidly comments that he was as well received at Court 'as if he had done excellent service' [19 Oct. 1627]. And for all the deficiencies of his account of the 1628-29 Parliament, Whiteway was clearly aware that something of wider significance was at stake than the specific issues of billeting, arbitrary imprisonment, and prerogative taxation. At the outset, he observes, the Commons 'began to vindicate their liberty', and when he gets to the stormy dissolution scene he describes

[15]

Sir John Eliot's three inflammatory resolutions as 'the three articles of liberty' [17 Mar. 1627/8; 20 Jan. 1628/9].

It is unlikely that many Dorchester people below Whiteway's social level were as politically well-informed as he was, and it may also be that he was unusual in the strength of his political beliefs. Both of the two contested county elections he mentions appear at first sight to have been of the old-fashioned kind; contests for pre-eminence among county families, with no visible ideological colouring [2 Feb. 1623/4; 30 Jan. 1625/6]. However, the long account of the 1626 election in his commonplace book suggests that it may not have been quite as simple as that. The losing candidate, John Browne of Frampton (defeated by the chicanery of the sheriff, Whiteway alleges) was living in Dorchester at the time, came of a family with moderately puritan sympathies, and was supported by several country gentlemen of similar views – Sir Richard Strode, Sir George and Sir Thomas Trenchard.[13] Whiteway's perception is that the voters from Dorchester formed something like a recognizable bloc – and Dorchester was already strikingly puritan in character by this time. Both groups agreed on one candidate, Sir Thomas Freke, but for the second place, Whiteway tells us, 'the Towne cried a Browne . . . and many of the Country did the same'; other rural voters who 'had beene before dealt withall underhand', shouted for his opponent, Sir George Moreton. The division may not have been explicitly political, but the possibility of a political or religious undercurrent cannot be ruled out.

Dorchester itself had by now abandoned the automatic acceptance of nominees from the Court or from patrons like the Earl of Bedford which had been the rule in Elizabethan days.[14] The courtier Sir Thomas Edmonds was elected in 1621 (he chose to sit elsewhere) but otherwise, with one exception, the borough's MPs in the 1620s were local men: the Recorder, Sir Francis Ashley, prominent merchants like Parkins, the Whiteways, Richard Bushrod, Edmund Dashwood, and John Hill. A few years later, in 1640, the Earl of Suffolk tried to foist an outsider friendly to the Court onto the town, but received the bland answer from the Corporation that by the constitution of the town only freemen could be elected. According to recent precedent this was just strictly true: in 1628 Denzil Holles, son of the Earl of Clare, who was Ashley's son-in-law and owned property in the town, had been admitted freeman on the very day of the parliamentary election.[15] Holles was soon to be notorious as one of the

[16]

members who forcibly held the Speaker down in the chair to prevent him from adjourning the House before Eliot's resolutions
could be put to the vote. The King promptly put him in the Tower,
but the Dorchester Corporation audaciously presented him with a
silver cup 'for his service done in the last Parliament' [29 Dec.
1629]. It is not hard to deduce on which 'side' in this increasingly
polarised situation the sympathies of Whiteway's fellow-burgesses
lay.

Whiteway devotes much space to English political developments, but he devotes as much, or more, to continental ones.
Dorchester may have been a hundred miles from London, but it
was no rural backwater. Its leading merchants, including the
Whiteways, traded extensively with France and other countries;
the diary is full of their mercantile affairs. Through business and
kinship ties they also had close connections with mercantile groups
in Weymouth, Exeter and other places, and were in the habit of
sending sons and apprentices to France to learn the language and
conduct business for them. The diarist was himself in France in
1616 and on at least one other occcasion.[16] Such journeys brought
some Dorchester men into very close contact with the bitter conflicts over religion that had been ravaging Europe for the previous
half-century and more. Whiteway's cousin Denis Bond long
remembered his father's stories of continental journeys, including
an incident at Rouen in 1572 when, as a young apprentice, he
narrowly escaped with his life from the St. Bartholemew massacre.
Bond himself was at St. Malo for six weeks in 1603, and lived
at Cadiz between 1605 and 1607. The diarist's own father was
taken prisoner in Normandy by the forces of the Catholic League
in 1590, and was in a French Gaol for a year before he was
ransomed.[17]

Hearing stories like these, doubtless often repeated, from their
parents, and absorbing the messages of Protestant nationalism
incessantly transmitted in church and school, it is not surprising
that many young Englishmen of the early seventeenth century
grew up with a highly polarized vision of their world.[18] William
Whiteway certainly did. His diary reflects a consciousness of living
in heroic times, at a critical stage in the great cosmic struggle between
Protestant good and Catholic evil, now reaching its climax in the
Thirty Years War. He had plentiful sources of news from kinsmen
and business associates, from the connections of friends in the

[17]

town (including the rector, John White), possibly also from news-letters (though he never mentions printed 'Mercuries', the only newspapers of the time, which carried only foreign news). He could fit it all into the frame-work provided by his education, by the sermons he regularly heard, and by his impressively wide reading. He had a large personal library (Dorchester also had a town library), and his commonplace book is full of lengthy notes on such works as Guicciardini's *History of Italy*, Holinshead's *Chronicle*, and histories of the Venetian and Dutch republics.[19]

Although Whiteway shows much interest in the affairs of other countries, particularly in the fate of the French Huguenots, he regarded Spain and her German Hapsburg allies as the ultimate enemies. Englishmen might have serious maritime and commercial disputes with the Protestant Dutch, but in the end only Spain stood to gain from them. In the early part of the Thirty Years War the Catholic Hapsburgs had driven James I's son-in-law, the Elector Frederick, out of Bohemia and the Palatinate, and by the mid-1620s the Protestant cause appeared to be on the point of collapse. Whiteway dutifully records the depressing story, and that of the feeble English interventions. But by 1631 there had emerged a new Protestant champion, Gustavus Adolphus of Sweden. In April 1631 a 'solemn private fast' was held in Dorchester 'for the good success of the King of Sweden', and thereafter Swedish victories are regularly noted in the diary [1 Apr. and 9 Sept. 1631; 6 Apr. and 6 Nov. 1632]. After Gustavus's death in November 1632, and more particularly after the Swedish defeat at Nordlingen two years later, the war lost whatever religious inspiration it had ever had; but Whiteway died too soon to be disillusioned.

European events had a direct impact on English politics, deepening the unease that many like Whiteway felt about royal policies. From the outset of the diary there are recurrent hints of disquiet at James I's supposedly pro-Spanish stance. The execution of Ralegh, for example, was 'much lamented' by Londoners, and many people were 'exceedingly sory' at the King's favour to Gondomar, the Spanish Ambassador [Nov 1618; Feb. 1620/1]. Most troubling of all, however, was the 'Spanish Match', the scheme to marry James's heir, Prince Charles, to the Infanta of Spain. Whiteway sporadically reports the progress of the negotiations in his usual neutral tone, but when Charles and Buckingham returned to England in October 1623, blazing with anger at their treatment in Madrid, he notes the joyful celebrations that occurred all over England. At Dorchester, as in other places, the bells were rung, and Denis Bond had the town cannon dragged outside the walls to fire a salute.[20] This did not end Whiteway's suspicions of Spanish influence, for as late as June 1634 he observed that 'the whole Court leans much to the Spanish party'.

Whiteway viewed all these controversies from an essentially religious perspective. He was not, by the standards of his time, a fanatic, and does not appear to have shared the obsessively introspective concern for his spiritual health manifested by some of his contemporaries.[21] He was healthily curious about the world around him, taking pleasure in sightseeing trips, interested in architecture and painting. When a French painter came to Dorchester, Whiteway was not content with passively sitting for his own portrait, but plied the painter with questions about mixing colours and other technicalities.[22] But he was a man of his time, and his world was inevitably a religious one.

We have seen how Whiteway's Protestant sympathies coloured his treatment of international affairs. His hostility to English Catholics is equally obvious. It is matched by a similar antipathy towards the Arminians, the newly emerging faction within the Church of England, who were attempting to shift the Church away from the moderately Calvinist position it had maintained ever since the Elizabethan settlement, in what conservative Protestants perceived as a distinctly 'popish' direction. Whiteway's alarm over Arminian influence first becomes apparent in 1627, when the moderate Archbishop Abbot was suspended and William Laud (who was to succeed him at Canterbury in 1633) became the King's most influential ecclesiastical advisor, and when the Calvinist royal chaplain, John Preston, was dismissed from Court 'for preaching plainly against Idolatry' – Whiteway's codeword for Arminianism. Thereafter his notices of the Arminians are invariably hostile, especially towards Laud. Arminianism, he noted in his commonplace book, was 'the mother of Atheism'.[23] And like many others of his time, he saw a clear connection between Arminianism and the authoritarian 'new counsels' now uppermost at Court. His version of the imprisonment of the Arminian Roger Mainwaring by Parliament in 1628 is that it was for his 'seditious speeches against the liberty of the subject' [14 Apr. 1628].

Does this mean that Whiteway was a 'puritan'? He would not

have accepted the label, and would have regarded it, as did everyone else in his period, as a divisive term of abuse.[24] But he shared many of the attitudes that have commonly been regarded as characteristically puritan: a preference for serious-minded preaching and the study and exposition of scripture, a preoccupation with sobriety and personal morality. His concern for 'godly reformation' is evident when he records the divine punishments visited on drunkards, participants in disorderly maypole festivities, and revellers on the sabbath, though in earlier days he could record a drinking-song without comment. He was much agitated by the great debate over Sunday recreations which culminated in the issue of Charles I's Book of Sports in 1633, a proclamation that outraged puritans and many other orthodox Protestants by its permissiveness. He reports (not very accurately) the initial stages of the controversy in Somerset, the widespread reluctance of the clergy to read the Book from their pulpits, as they were commanded to do, and the subterfuge by which the Dorchester churchwardens protected their formidably uncompromising rector, John White, in 1634, on the eve of the Metropolitan Visitation. His concern is also shown by the series of 'Questions concerning the L[ord's] day' which he entered in his commonplace book.[25]

Whether or not we describe Whiteway as a puritan is largely a matter of semantics. We need not accept Archbishop Laud's definition, by which all critics of Arminian innovations were categorized as such, for those critics not unreasonably regarded themselves as upholding the true, orthodox traditions of the English church. Still, the programme of civic improvement that Dorchester was pursuing in the early seventeenth century was also a programme of moral improvement – of 'godly reformation' – and its inspiration can only be described as puritan, if the term has any meaning at all.

The campaign had begun immediately after the arrival of John White as rector in 1605, and was supported by influential members of the old town elite as well as by newcomers like the Bonds and Whiteways. At first they made little headway, but after the great fire of August 1613 the situation changed dramatically. Whiteway saw the disaster as a major turning-point. Before the fire, he later recalled, 'littel or no mony was given to any charitable uses for a long season, men lay frozen in the dreggs untill it pleased God to awaken them by this fyrye triall'.[26] The programme of reformation that ensued – social, educational, and religious reformation – made Dorchester within a few years perhaps the most puritan town in England. We should not forget that John White and his allies regarded themselves as nothing more than orthodox, conforming members of the true, Protestant Church of England, fighting the eternal struggle with evil in all its forms. But it was fortunate for them that successive bishops of Bristol, in whose diocese Dorchester lay, were moderates, not Laudian persecutors. Even so, on several occasions it was touch and go whether White would be suspended: notably in 1634 over the Book of Sports, and again in 1635-1636 when he was summoned before the Court of High Commission.[27] The struggle to make Dorchester a reformed 'city on a hill' was at the very heart of William Whiteway's mental and spiritual world. It is the constant, though often unspoken, accompaniment to his diary.

REFERENCES

1 See, for example, John Morrill, *The Revolt of the Provinces* (1976), pp. 21-8.
2 Cambridge University Library, MS Dd. xi. 73: Whiteway's Commonplace Book, fols. 43v-4.
3 I am grateful to Sarah Bridges for this information.
4 Commonplace Book, fols. 43v-7. Whiteway's kinsman Denis Bond kept an even more elaborate chronology: Dorset Record Office, D 413/22/1 (another copy in D 53/1).
5 References to the diary are hereafter given in this form, in square brackets in the text.
6 For Wallington, see Paul S. Seaver, *Wallington's World: A Puritan Artisan in Seventeenth-Century London* (Stanford, Cal., 1985).
7 Dorset Record Office, D1/JC8: 'William Whiteway's Book', 1625 (another copy in D1/10,448).
8 R. C. Johnson, M. F. Keeler, M. J. Cole, et al., *Proceedings in Parliament 1628* (New Haven, 1977-83), II, 361.
9 *Calendar of State Papers, Domestic, 1628-9*, pp. 101-2, 131.
10 See Richard Cust, *The Forced Loan and English Politics 1626-1628* (Oxford, 1987).
11 Organized opposition in Parliament was a concept totally foreign to this period: Conrad Russell, *Parliaments and English Politics 1621-1629* (Oxford 1979).
12 fols. 67v-9, 153.
13 Commonplace Book, fols. 149-51.

14   P. W. Hasler, *The House of Commons 1558-1603* (1981), I, 151-2.
15   C. H. Mayo (ed.), *The Municipal Records of the Borough of Dorchester* (Exeter, 1908), pp. 395, 435.
16   Commonplace Book, fol. 45.
17   Bond's Chronology (D 413/22/1), pp. 34-7. Whiteway's Commonplace Book, fol. 44.
18. Oliver Cromwell, it might be noted, was born in 1599, the same year as Whiteway.
19   Commonplace Book, fols. 8-11, 39-40, 175-83v. For the town library, see Mayo, *Municipal Records*, pp. 581-3.
20   Bond's Chronology (D 413/22/1), p. 44.
21   Nehemiah Wallington, for example: see above, n. 4.
22   Commonplace Book, fols. 23-8, 32-4 (the book also contains many architectural drawings). See also Diary, 15 Oct. 1633.
23   Diary, 12 July and Dec. 1627; Commonplace Book, fol. 183.
24   Christopher Hill, *Society and Puritanism in Pre-Revolutionary England* (2nd edn., 1972), ch. 1.
25   Commonplace Book, fols. 42v-3. For the whole issue, see David Underdown, *Revel, Riot, and Rebellion: Popular Politics and Culture in England 1603-1660* (Oxford, 1985), pp. 65-7.
26   'William Whiteway's Book" (D1/JC8), p. 2. For Dorchester during this period, see Frances Rose-Troup, *John White, the Patriarch of Dorchester* (1930). I hope to discuss the puritan campaign and its impact on Dorchester in a forthcoming book.
27   Rose-Troup, *John White*, pp. 295-304. Whiteway's entry for 1 June 1630 may refer to another such occasion, though it is possible that by 'removing' he means removal to another parish, or perhaps even into New England.

THE DIARY

1618

1618
In the sixteenth yeare of the Raigne of our Soveraigne Lord James by the grace of god, King of England, france, and Ireland Defendour of the Faith and of Scotland the two and Fiftieth.

Sir Walter Earle knight was sheriffe of Dorset.

John Gould and William Jolliffe Bailives of Dorchester.

John Hill and Dionis Bond Constables.

Aetatis mei 19.[1]

November 1618
There was seene a Blazing Star in the South East, which continued.[2]

Sir walter Rawleigh was beheded in London about the end of October and after his Death was much Lamented by the Londiners, having acquitted himselfe of the Death of the Earle of Essex, and of his Atheisme; as appeareth by his speech at his Execution.[3]

About the same tyme also their were many reports of warres betwixt England and France, and the Low Countreyes, but no certeinty in any of them. The ground onely was because their was no English Ambassador in France, nor French in England.

De Ill[ustrissi]mo Equite Gualtero Rawleigh
Epig[ramma] D[omini] R. Bechi Durotrigis
Poe[tae] Laureati.

[*Concerning the most illustrious knight Walter Raleigh, epigram of the Revd. R. Beech, Poet Laureate of Dorchester*]

Once he was Grace itselfe
And could make other gratious.
Envie that crooked Elfe
Thought that life was to spatious.

[23]

And therefore did confine him
Into a narrower place
Where she meant to assigne him
The dregs of all disgrace.

But vertue then provided
Sorting his Fortunes so
That they should be divided,
Some good with bad to goe.

And in despight of Envies face,
To live and dy, grac't in disgrace.

After his execution he was much Lamented, to cleare Justice, the Kings Majesty wrote a booke concerning him.

10 December
We heard by Mr Sambourne that the king of France his second sister should be married to the Duke of Savoy his sonne.

We heard allso that the Lord Cardinal du Perron, (who was the son of a Protestant Minister) was dead, and that upon his Death-bead he sent for a Minister, and Recanted his Relligion, dying a Protestant. The Jesuites that were about him, after his Death did so corrupt the aforesaid Minister with guifts and promises of preferment, that he is turned Papist. Which they did, fearing to be disgraced. This I heard of a Gentleman comming from Wareham.

20 December
It was Reported that there was great stir in Bohemia about choosing them a king, who it is hoped shalbe a Protestant, which may be a meanes to bring in a Protestant Emperour in Germany. And afterwards we heard that the Elector Palatin, son in Law to the King of England, is like to be chosen king.

1619

1 January 1618/19
We heard that their was a very great Armada provided in Spaine,
but it is Not yet knowne for what Country. It is reported to Be greater
then that in 88.

4 January

Come discontented thoughts, take up your seate
In his sad soule, that daily feeds on you,
And whose sad soule, you sowerly doe eate,
Changing red cheekes to pale, red lips to Blew.
Stand close, as you do use, and heare me mourne
Or els, my Smothered greiffe, my heart will Burne.

When I can find but one good in this life,
Which is to trust entirely upon god,
When all things els, yeeld me but paine and Greiffe,
And nought appeares to me, but seemes a Rod.
Tell me (my Deare Companions) how I may
If not extinguish, yet my greiffe Allay.

Ile to the wildernes Betake my selfe,
Ile never pare my nailes, nor cut my haire.
Ile make the earth my house, Bord, bed, and shelfe,
Ile passe my life (to this world) in Dispaire.
Untill I see change in Aristo's Carriadge.
And Be assur'd to have my Love in Marriage.[4]

5 January
I heard that the King of Spain had disclaymed the supremacy of
the Pope. That the Duke of Guise in France, had vowd the taking of
Argier in Barbary, as allso that the Low Country men provided a
fleet of 50 saile to set upon the King of Spaine his treasure, comming
from the west Indies.

16 January
It was reported, that Sir Lewys Stukely, Vice Admiral of Devon,
who had the charge of Sir walter Rawleigh when he was prisoner,

[25]

having [Received] mony for betraying him, fell to clypping the Gold, and is thereupon apprehended.

In this moneth the King his Banquetting house at the Palace of Whitehall was Burnt, and the 29th dicto Sir Thomas Smith his house at Detford nere London was Burnt, lying next to the Kings storehouse for Cordage.

The 2nd March Queene Anne of England, Sister to Christian, King of Denmarke, died about 4 a Clocke in the Morning.

3 March
It was said that Matthias themperour of Germany and the Empresse were dead.

23 July 1619
                    Nondum satis.

[*The remainer of this page and the next page have been obliterated; the writing appears to be verse.*]

28 August
The Lottery for the Virginia Company began to be opened, consisting of 50000 blancs, 1750 prices worth £1259 for one shilling a Lotte.

Ferdinand, Duke of Gretes, and that was chosen heretofore King of Bohemia, was chosen Emperour of Germany, to the great Greiffe of the Poore Protestants of that Countrey.[5]

In this Moneth: there was established a Custome upon all wooll cloth, being on our Dorsetts 9d a [?Cloth] more then Before and 6d on a Devon. What wilbe the Issue of it is not yet knowen.

29 September
The kingdome of Bohemia being void by the death of the Late Emperour Matthias, the estates of the Country with one Consent chose Fredericke Prince elector Palatine, and Lady Elisabeth his wife, King and Queene of Boheme, who were Crowned at Prage upon Michaelmas day. Whereupon the Pope and Emperour tooke up Armes, and amongst others had the overthrow, Bucquoy, being Generall of their Army, in which battell were slaine 2000 of the Palsgraves side, and 5000 of the other.

1619

1 October

Mr John Parkins was chosen to his third Bailliwicke. Mr William Horsford his partner to his second.

Mr dionis bond Constable with mr John Cooke, and Matthew Buttler Shoomaker, being the first yeare that we had three Constables.

Being Tuesday about 10 of the Clocke at night, I had a Brother Borne, was Baptised by the Name of James, and named so by mr John Hill and mr Richard Savidge, and my Aunt Pitt of Bridport.

NEL KORO SENZA PAR [*Without equal in the chorus.*]

November

My Lord of Suffolke, Late Lord Treasurer, for abusing his office was fined in £100000 some say, but £30000 and Imprisonment during the Kings pleasure.

His daughter the Lady Car died prisoner in the Tower. Sir Anthony Aishley was chosen sheriffe of Dorsett, being an ancient gentleman and knightd in Calis Action by the Earle of Essex for his Valour.

He chose for his undersheriff mr John Cole the yonger of Piddletowne – price £100.

We heard that the Prince of Condé who had beene reported to have beene dead, was sett at liberty againe, having beene kept prisoner in the Bastill at Paris 3 or 4 year.

[*Entry obliterated*]

December 10. We heard that the Archduke of Austria Albertus was Dead and Leopoldus his Brother made Archduke in his Stead.

[*Remainder of the page obliterated*]

[27]

1620

5 January 1619/20

We heard that the Marques of Buckingham was Created Duke of Buckingham and the Earle of Arundelle Duke of Norfolke, as allso that the family of the Howards goes downe a pace as in the Earle of Suffolke, and his heire the Lord Walden, who is put out of his place of Captain of the Pensioners.

26 February

My little Brother James deceased being not yet ½ a yeare old.

The beginning of this yeare was very sickily for all sorts of persons, especially of young children. Wherof there have died since the first of January a great Number.

March 1620

There was by order from the King a Drumme beaten in London for all Voluntaries to the number of 2000 that would goe to the succor of the King of Bohemia. Which number was afterwards made up and led by Sir Horatio Veer, Lord Generall, with whome went the Earle of Oxford and the Earle of Essex, 2 hopefull Noble Men.

26 March

The King, Prince, and a great part of the Nobility came to Poules in London to heare a sermon, and to see the Ruines of that Church; to the Repairing whereof his Majesty hath promised to be a royall Benefactor.

At this time there was in London an extraordinary Embassador from Spaine to treat about the Marriage as some say Betwixt the 2 kinges. Which is since reported to be broken of, the Prince standing upon it, that he will Treat of a Match for himselfe.

6 Aprill

Was concluded the Marriage betwixt me William Whiteway and Elenor Parkins my best beloved, which I pray god to blesse and prosper.

[28]

4 May
The said W. W. and E. P. were betrothed in my father Parkins his
hall about 9 of the Clocke at night by mr John White, in the presence of our Parents, Unkle John Gould and mr Darby and their
wives, my Cossen Joan Gould widow, and my sister Margaret
Parkins etc.

14 June
I William Whiteway was married to Elenor Parkins by mr John
White in the Church of the holy Trinity in Dorchester, in the
presence of the greatest part of the Towne, which marriage I pray
god to Blesse, that it may turne to his glory, and our good, and the
Comfort of all our freinds. Amen.

The wedding Ring had this Posy:
Conjugii firmi, et casti sum pignus amoris.
[*I am the pledge of a steadfast marriage and of chaste love.*]

About this time of the yeare their began to be stirs in france. The
Queene Mother and the Princes disdaining that the king should be
so much governed by a man of so small birth as his favorit M[onsieur]
de luynes is, departed from the Court, and raisd an army, did for-
tify themselves in Many places in Normandy against the King who
Came with an army to Rouen, and thence went to Caen and by his
presence disperst the Troubles, and tooke the Castle of Caen after
3 daies which was one of their Cheife holds. But all was not so
blowne over, for the Troubles were remooved from there up into
the heart of france, about Tours.

The end of this moneth, Sir Horatio Veer, with his brave troope
sett forward towards Bohemia, from whence we had newes that the
Imperialls had a great overthrow, wherein the generall Conte
Bucquoy was Slayne flying over a Mote.

July
Our king and Prince began their Progress into the west in this
Moneth and the 1st of August Came to Sarum and the 12th thereof
to Cranborne, upon the Plaine.

In this moneth their were a Company of drunkards assembled in
Hamshire, who hanged up one of their Companions by the wast,
and powred drinke into his mouth, so that they killed him with itt.
And neare that tyme and Place another dranke himselfe starke
dead, a Gentelman.

1

The blacke Jacke, the merry blacke Jacke
As it is tost on hy a.
Growes – flowes – till at last the[y] fall to blowes
And make their Noddles cry a.

2

The browne bowle, The merry browne bowle
As it goes Round about a.
Fill – Still – let the world say what it will
And drinke the drinke all out a.

3

The deepe Can. The merry deepe Can.
As we do freely quaffte a
Fling – Sing – Be as merry as a king
And Sound a lusty laugh a.

τεχνογαμιά
[*Marriage of skills?*]

The troubles before mentioned in france were Composed in August, the Queene mother, Received into favour and all things pacified but the Armyes were not dismissd which they said the King meant to Lead into the Country of Bearne.

29 September
There were chosen Burgesses of
Dorchester Bailiffs for this yeare
    Mr William Whiteway 3.
    Mr Edmond Dashwood 2.
Constables.   Sheriffe of Dorset.
    Mr John Cooke.   Sir Nathaniel Napper, Knight.
    Mr John Blachford.   Undersheriffe.
    Christopher Way.   Mr Newman of Fiford.

[October]
About this time of the yeare we had many reports out of Germany. The truest are these, that Themperor being put [out] by his kingdome of Boheme, published a ban Inciting all the Princes of the Empire to assist him for the Recovery thereof, which some doe and some refuse. The Dukes of Saxony and of Bavaria are for the Emperor with others. The estates for the king of Bohemia, and the King of Hungary. Betthlem Gabor is his great freind, who doth

1620

assist him very much. In Austria and there about are great troubles. Many Conflicts ther have beene, with diverse event. In one, Tampire, one of the Emperors Generalls was shot through the head with a Musquet, and after his body beheaded, caryed away by the enemyes and put to Ransome, but Buquoy is not slayne though it was so reported. The King of Bohemia himselfe is in the field with about 40000 men ready to fight, upon any occasion.

In the Palatinat Spinola leads an army for the King of Spaine and hath taken in it 4 townes, but the report is, that since, he is glad to retire to ments. The Prince of Orange fortifieth there abouts.

On this moneth set to sea the great fleet of 20 great ships, 6 of the Kings and 14 merchant ships, for the Pyrats at Alguers it was thought they had some other Intent. They had 2 Commissions one to be opend at Plimmouth, the other at the Souther Cape of Spaine. What will become of them, we shall shortly heare.

27th of this October. Mr Attorney Generall Sir Henry yelverton was Censured in Star Chamber, for granting some priviledge to the Citty of london without the kings knowledge. This Censure is referred to the King. They say The Lord Cheiffe Justice Sir Henry Montague is made Lord Treasurer. So he is.

1 November
There is a Parlement determind to be held upon the 16th day of January next.

In this moneth was there a free Collection made for the defence of the Palatinat and in Dorchester was given £200. The Papists have Collected in England for the Emperor £30000 whereof part is fallen into his Majestyes hands, the rest like to be discovered.

3rd Dicto fu fatto dalcuni di questa villa un solenne digiuni, con lunghe orationi in favore dei Boemi: et La prima di December Il medesmo fu pratticata in caussa medesma. [*3rd Dicto there was held by some of this household (or town) a solemn fast with long prayers on behalf of the Bohemians, and the first of December the same was carried out in the same cause.*]

29 November
There Came newes to the towne that the King of Bohemia was overthrowen by Count Bucquoy and fled with the Queene Into

Silesia, and that the Duke of Bavaria, and Bucquoy comming to Prague, had it yeelded up to them in which the souldiers behaved themselves so Insolently that after they had pilled the citty 3 times in seven daies, the townsmen rose, and drave them out and kept the towne for the king of Bohemia. But of the trueth of this Last Part it is uncerteyne.

12 December
Were chosen here the knights of the Parlement for Dorsett. Sir John Strangewaies, and Sir Thomas Trenchard. For Dorchester were chosen Burgesses Sir Francis Aishley, Sergeant at Law, and mr John Parkins. For Waymouth and Melcombe videlicet Mr John Freake and mr Christopher Earle gentelmen and Mr Matthew Pitt, and mr Giles Greene Tounesmen. For Bridport Mr John Stroud, and mr John Browne Esquires. For Lyme Mr John Paulet Esquire and Mr John Hazard Gentelman.

29 December
There arrived at london a great nobleman of France, Embossadour from the french king, le Marquis de Cadenet, Mareshall of france, elder brother to the Duc de luynes the king of France his favorit. He was enterteyned with very great Pompe, having 35 coaches sent to conduct him to London and is Logded in Somerset alias Denmarke house. What his message is time will make knowne.

About this tyme the king of france threatned the Protestants to roote them out and to Beseige Rochelle for not admitting him into their citty with all his troupes. Which they did, fearing least they should be used as the Bearnois were, who having given him entrance, upon the faith of a king, when he was entred, seased of their forts and sett over them Popish Governors and gave their Ministers Lands to Priests and Jesuits.

1621

The Parlament was prorogued from the 16th of January unto the 23th thereof.

3 January 1620/1
There came into the Countrey a Proclamation to forbid all men to Speake of matters of State, either of this kingdom or of any other Place, upon pain of his Majesties high displesure.

13 January
Sir Francis Aishley who had beene chosen Burgesse of Parliament for Dorchester, resigned over his place unto Sir Thomas Edmonds knight of his Majesties privy Counsell and Steward of his Majesties house, who had Laine Embassador at the french Court many yeares.

The Parliament was againe proroged from the 23th January for 6 daies Longer and began upon the 30th day of this moneth. Wherein his Majesty made a Learned discourse unto the whole house of the cause of assembling them, whereof he made 3 parts. The first was the want of mony. The second, to give unto them all satisfaction concerning the mariage of the Prince, who he hoped should never match, but to the honour of Religion and advancement thereof. The last, was to Informe them of his risolution touching the wars of Germany, that he never approoved the war of Bohemia, but for the Palatinat, which the Spaniards goe about to deprive his Son in Law frederike of, he would Imploy all his forces to recover it and some reported that their should be a levy made of twenty five thousand men for that service.

February
About the 22th day of January Last the weather grew extreame cold and continued so untill the 5th day of this moneth, at what tyme it grew milder. But within one day it resumed his former extremity, and so Continued 6 dayes longer.
Mrs Elenor Chappell of Exon, my granmother died the 1 day of

[33]

february leaving her whole estate unto her son Richard the younger, who died 8 dais after and left his estate all to his wife.

15th dicto forty Lords of Parliament and foureskore burgesses presented unto the King a Petition, for the restrayning of the liberty that Papists and Jesuits have, who answered them, that he knewe better how to governe then they could teach him, that hereby he should moove other Princes to deale more violently with Protestants, but that he left them to be proceeded against by his laws.

The 40 and 80 aforesaid did beseech his Majesty to recall a Commysion granted to the Spanish Ambassador for the shipping away of 100 tons of Iron Ordynance. But received this answere, that he had given him the faith and word of a King, and therefore could not recall it, which 2 things made a great many to be exceeding sory.

It was reported by diverse that the Fort of Gibraltar within the mouth of the Streights was taken by the Hollanders men of war that ly there about for the suppressing of Pirats.

1 March
This day began the Assises for this County, held by Justice Hutton alone, the rest of the Judges being Imploied at the Parliament.

9 March
Sir francis Aishley who had beene first chosen Burges for the Parliament was againe chosen, Sir Thomas Edmondes being before chosen for another place. In the meane time the Parliament was continued this whole moneth, to the great content both of the King and the subjects, wherein first to testify their love unto him, they granted him two subsidies to be collected in Aprill. From thence they proceeded to reforme such greivances as were presented against the Lord Chancellor, Sir Francis Bacon, Vicont of Saint Albanes, and some other great men. They called in and condemned all Monopolies especially that for Innes and Alehouses and for making of Venice gold. Which were granted unto Sir Giles Mompesson who mistrusting himselfe, fled out of his keepers hands, and is Censured now £10000 fine, his Lands forfeited, himselfe ignoble, degraded of his knighthood and banished his Majesties Dominions. Sir francis Michel a partner of his is sent to the Tower and from thence to Newgate. Mr Shepheard a Burgesse is excluded the house for casting upon another Burgesse the name of

Puritan. Many have been excluded the house for being Papists. In searching out of Abuses they have come very neare to some great men, which is not yet ended. They have concluded yet but few Acts. One against Drunkennesse, another to settle Lands upon Hospitalls. Finally upon the 28th March 1621 the Parliament was adjourned unto the 17th Aprill.

During this moneth their was great preparation for war made in moste parts of Christendome. The 12 years truce betwixt Spaine and the States of the Low Countreyes, ending the 9th day of Aprill this yeare, novo stilo. The States have 60000 men, 10000 marryners, such mony, and shipping ready and will not harken to any peace, but upon very good Termes.

In Germany the Princes of the Union stand to defend themselves, against whome the Emperor doth prosecute his Imperiall Banne by all meanes. The King of Denmarke armes in behalfe of the King of Bohemia. Spinola and Bucquoy have beene doing, but without any great matters of Importance. The Hollanders waite to Intercept the 120 tons of great ordinance that was sent for Spaine, which is not yet past the British Ocean.

1 Aprill 1621
This day died Philip 3 king of Spaine having the day before proclaimed warre against the Lowe Countreyes, to whome succeeded his Sonne King Philip 4 aged now about 18 yeeres.

About this tyme also died the little old Earle of Hartford, as also Dr King, Bishop of London, a man of Excellent learning, and great Integrity.

About this tyme was Monsieur de luines the french kings favorit, made the great Conestable of france, with great disdaine of the other Princes.

The 6th hereof was a great tumult among the Apprentices of London about the Spanish Ambassador, so that the King, and all the Court did take knowledge of the matter, and caused one of them to be whipt about the streets, guarded with 200 halbards.

The 10th hereof the countrey began to Levy the Subsidy granted unto the King by the house of Parliament. At the adjourning

whereof his Majesty made a gratious speech unto them, Exhorting
them to goe forward in execution of Justice, and withall knighted
the speaker Sir Richard Richardson, Sergeant at Law. And at this
tyme came down 3 Proclamations against three [of] the great
Monopolyes and for the Banishment of Giles Mompesson, who
was by them called the Lord of hostes.

15 Aprill
This day was my father-in-law mr John Parkins married in Exon to
a widow in Exon Mrs Rachel Chappell, she being his second wife,
and he her third husbande.

At this tyme their was a great falling out at Paris betwixt the duke
of Guise and his side, and the Duke of Nevers, upon a box on the
eare given him by the said Duke of Guise. Which put the Court in
uprore.

Memorandum. This winter and spring all sort of corne was at a
low price, wheate was sold for 20d and 2s with us, barley for 16d,
oates for 10d, ry for 16d, but towards somer the price began to rise
againe.

11 May
Being friday about eight of the clocke in the morning the sunne was
Eclipsed, the moone Covering the midst of it and a golden circle
appearing round about it.

The 17 hereof the Parliament was adjorned untill the 24th of the
same moneth, having in the former session pronounced sentence
against sir francis Bacon, Lord Chancelor, Baron of Verulam and
Vicont of St Albons, for his extreme Bribery, putting him from his
place, fined him in £40000 sterling and perpetuall imprisonment,
during the Kings pleasure.

Sir francis Michel being one of Sir Giles Mompesson his Consorts
was sent unto finsbury Jaile, a place made by him for Rogues, and
made to ride on a leane jade backeward through london, holding
the tail in his hand having a Paper upon his forehead, wherein was
written his offence. And the 18th of this moneth Sir Henry yelverton,
Attorney Generall was called to answer to such things as were
objected against him, and then had 6 daies respite given him, which
the Earle of Arundell did dislike, whereupon the Lord Spenser
said That the Lord of Arundels predcessors had beene censured

there for treason before their tyme, and therefore were offended. Then said the Earle, my predecessors sate here, while yours did keepe sheepe, and upon that he was commanded to goe to the bar and crave pardon of the Lord Spenser, which he refusing was sent away to the Tower. And Sir Henry Yelverton in his answere offers to proove, that wherein he had offended was upon The Lord Marquis of Buckinghams letters.

In this season the King of france proceeded to set forward towards Rochell and in the meane tyme, disarmed the Protestants in Rouen, Caen, Deipe, Newhaven, and other places of Normandy, the Duke of Longuevill being governour.

The young king of Spaine and his yonger Brother were at Variance about the Kingdome of Portugall, which they say the old King bequethed unto his second sonne, and besides hath donne many things that for his age seeme strange. Among the rest, he hath turned out of favor his fathers cheife favorites.

[June]
The 4th hereof the Parliament was adjourned untill the 14th day of November next, and at breaking up their Session they all made a protestation to dy in the Palsgraves quarrell if need were.

The 11th hereof my wife was delivered of a mayde childe about ½ an houre after eleven a clocke at night. She was baptised the 17th thereof and called Mary by my unkle mr John Gould Senior, my owne mother and my mother in Law Mrs Rachel parkins. God Blesse her.

Memorandum. Mr John Churchel Esquire died the 1st of June and was buryed the 7th in St Peters in Dorchester aged about 50 yeares or upwards.

In this moneth the french king laid seige to St John d'Angely, and had it at last yelded by Composition, but hee kept not his word towards them. Saulmur and some other places did Receive him and had new Governors. Rochelle is not yet beseiged, but they and all that favour them are proclaimed traitors if they doe refuse to take the oath ministred unto them on the Kings behalfe, that they shall in no sort assist those that stand out against the King. Whereupon divers especially their Ministers have forsaken their Countrey, many are come into England. And this hath mooved the

Rochellers to stand stoutly in their owne defence; and to send unto
the King of England for aide. In the meane tyme they make prize of
all that they can take by sea. Before St John d'angely, died in the
King of france his army, the Cardinal de Guise, the two Mareschals
of Brissac and Vitry of the bloody flux as is reported. Hereupon the
King set forward towards Burdeaux for what intent is not to us
knowen.

In this moneth there was great adoe at the Court of England. The
Earle of Southampton, Sir Edwyne Sands, and mr Seldyn were
committed to Custody, as it is thought for meeting with many other
noblemen and Gentlemen at thearle of dorsets house in London,
to Confer of some good Course for their owne safety. Their was
great changing of Bishops. Dr Mountain bishop of Lincolne was
made Bishop of London, and Dr Williams Deane of Westminster
φιλανακτόφιλος [*friend of the friends of those in high places*]
was made Bishop of Lincolne; and many others of which we
heare not.

The report was that Sir francis Bacon Lord Chancelor vicont St
Albones was to be made Lord Deputy of Ireland. [*This entry has been
crossed through.*]

July
July 12th beganne th'assiss for Dorsett holden before Sir Lawrence
Tanfield, Lord Cheife Baron and Sir Richard Hutton, Justice for
the King.

This sommer was finished the stately Banqueting house at
Whitehall all built of Portland stone, which had beene burnt downe
in January anno 1618.

In the midst of this moneth were committed to prison th'earle of
Oxford and Dr Baily, bishop of Bangor; and shortly after were released againe together with the earle of Southampton and those
that were laid up with him. The earle of Northumberland was also
then delivered out of the Tower who had beene their a long tyme
and Sir Henry yelverton. The earle of Somerset was likely also to
have been delivered at that tyme; what was the cause of these mens
Imprisonment is not knowne.

The 21th hereof. The Lord Haies Viscont Doncaster went ambassador into france upon the suite of the Rochellers to treate with the

french king about the poore Protestants. Whome the Jesuites under him doth persecute most furiously.

About this tyme died the Archduke Albertus of the low Countryes. And it was reported that Count Bucquoy was Slayne with a musket shot as he went to view Newsoll to beseige it, and that Count Mansfelt gave unto the Imperialls a great overthrow, but my Lord Digby is at the Emperors Court to Labour for a peace.

August
16th hereof died mr William Horsford one of the Aldermen of this towne, and in his roome was chosen mr Barnard Toope. Upon the 29th of the same, died mr Richard Barker, alderman, and in his place was chosen Mr Dionis Bonde to make up the nomber.[6]

At this time returned part of the fleete out of the Streights that set to Sea in October last. 8 are allready come, the rest are comming after, but have not performed any great service.

About the end of this moneth, Lowys Duke of Lennox married with the Lady Francis Countesse of Harford. [*The remaining words of this entry are obliterated.*]

11 September
This was a very cold and moist Sommer which ripened corne but slowly, so that it began to rise at harvest, which was very late, their being corne in the fields till the 10th of October. It was also a very great yeare of Plums, so that a pecke were sold for a penny.

In this moneth the King of france having taken St Jean d'Angely, went and beseiged Mountauban, a place of the Relligion, where he lay a long time with 40 tons of ordinance, to the losse of many of his men. At last hee was overthrowen by the Protestants, lost 1500 men, and among the rest De luynes, De maine, and de guise, Dukes. And it is reported that Caen was lately like to have beene surprised by the Protestants.

October 2nd were chosen Bailiffs for Dorchester.
Mr Richard Blachford.
Mr Richard Bushrod 2.
Constables.
John Blachford.
Christopher way.
John Long.

Governor.
Mr John hill.
Sheriffe of Dorset.
Sir Edward Lawrence, Knight.
Undersheriffe.
Mr Richard May, Gentleman.

This same day came downe certain Commissioners with the broad seale of England, to dig in a hill at Upway neare Dorchester, for some treasure that lyes hidden under ground; but having spent three daies about it they went away, having found there nothing but a few bones, saying they went to digge at Bincombe, but under that pretence went cleane away.

Sir Lionel Cranfield, Lately made Lord Cranfield, was made now Lord Treasurer, and the former Viscont Mandeville, was made Lorde president of the counsell, which place wilbe shortly due to our Noble Prince Charles, who in November next wilbe 21 yeares old.

At Corke in Ireland, two flockes of Stares came over the town, and there fought a great battell, so that a great number of them fell downe dead in the streets, some say 20000 (which is not credible). Some had their bills broken, their leggs, their eyes put out. Malum omen avertat deus. [*May God avert the bad omen.*]

The Turke being come into Polonia with 300000 fighting men about this time fought a great battell with the Polonians, and therein lost 170000 Men. Yet for all that he got the Victory over them, drave them out of the field, slew the King of Polonia, Sigismund and his son, and are like to overrunne all Polonia, while the Emperour and German Princes are at variance, and so make way unto him to seize on all.

Dr George Abbots Archbishopp of Canterbury, having in hunting shot a man by chance in the arme with a crossebow about 3 or 4 monethes since, whereof he died, was found irregular, and thereupon remooved from his place, and in his steed came Dr Andrewes, Bishop of Ely, Quondam. This report prooved quite false.

Uppon a report of Shipping to be provided to suppresse the Insolency of the Hollanders this was found in London.

> The Belgic frog
> Out of the Bog
> with the British mouse did strive
> Th' Iberian Kite
> meane while by sleight
> surpriseth both alive.
>
> While for their shares
> of Indian wares
> English and Dutch do brawle,

The Spaniard watcheth,
advantage catcheth
To seize on them and all.

Then be agreed,
And take good heede,
Make not a needless fray,
Least to a third,
That Ravenous Bird,
You both become a pray.

This also was found cast about the court, a while after
A. B. C. D. will bring in Popery.

The Rochelers about this time gave the king of france his fleete a great overthrow, tooke and burnt many of their ships. Amongst the rest they tooke the Admirall and Viceadmirall prisoners, and have taken this Sommer above 140 french ships.

Count Mansfield came into the Palatinat, and joyned with Sir Horace Vere, and the Duke Brunswicke, and gave Spinolas forces a great overthrow.

14 November
The Parliament which was adjorned to this day, was further adjourned to the 8th february. But upon my Lord Digbyes comming home, who could make no peace abroad, it was suddainly called to begin upon the 20th of this moneth.

[*Here a hand points to the previous entry, followed by an entry completely obliterated.*]

10 December
About this time the great Favorit and Constable of France, Charles Duke de Luynes, and Peere of France, died. The seige of Montauban being raised some 14 daies before, wherein the King lost about 20000 men and many Gunnes.

The Parliament having consulted a while about matters of State, sent a Peticion to the king about the Match, and wars with Spaine, but the king, informed thereof, forbad them to send it. Whereupon they sent another by 12 of their house, which his Majesty received and answered that the match with Spaine was concluded, and to advise them not to meddle with matters of State, till they were called to it, telling them that their priviledgs depended upon

[41]

his grace, and willing them to consult about making lawes, which they refused to doe untill their requests were granted. Whereupon on the 19th hereof the Parliament was adjourned unto the 8th february.

The 20th hereof died Mr John Yeate, one of the Aldermen of this Towne, very old, in whose Roome was chosen Mr John Hill, Ironmonger.

This same day fire brake out in Chancery Lane in London, by the negligence of a Clarke, and burnt 10 houses, with a great number of Records, and two Lords houses, but went no further.

1622

January 1621/2

The 5th hereof the Parliament, which had beene adjourned untill February, was by Proclamation cleane dissolved, his Majesty being offended with their Proceedings. And soone after Sir Edward Cooke was sent prisoner to the Tower, for maintaining the privileges of the house, and a little after him Sir Robert Philips.

The 9th hereof his Majesty wente from London to Theobalds, where riding into his parke with some keepers to see the Deere, being upon the ice, it brake, and his horse fell backeward into the water, and the King all under water, was drawen out by the legs, lay speechless for an hower, having received much water into his mouth, but is now well recovered, god be praised.

3 February

Mr Blanchard the Minister of Condé in Normandy, being refuged into England during the troubles in France, began to preach in the French tongue in his house admitting such to heare him as would come, whose audience increased every day, by meanes of his teaching the French tongue.

Robert Car, Earle of Somerset, was set at liberty out of the tower, where he had beene Prisoner 4 or five yeares, about the death of Sir Thomas Overbury etc.

About this time the king demanded a Benevolence, whereto all the Aldermen of London gave £100 a peice, and the rest of the Cittizens were taxed about the rate of 10 subsidies.

At this time also trades being very bad for Germany, their were certyn Clothiers in wilshire and Glostershire that went and demanded mony and meate violently of the Gentlemen of the Countrey. Which being reported to the privy Counsell, they compelled the London merchants to by cloth to mend the Trade.

A Tailor accompted distracted came the 18th february, crying through our Streets, woe, woe, to Rome that bloody citty, and many other woes to divers other persons, but especially unto Papists and

1622

Jesuits, who had done the same throughout London, yet none hindered him! He saith he was commanded to doe it by one that met him in a red cap. The Tailor was called Speering.

In the beginning of this moneth their came downe three of the kings ships, and three merchant ships from London, in which was the Earle of Oxford, to set upon and take Holland East India ships newly arrived at Plymouth, for whose succor there came also 6 men of war out of Holland, to garde them home.

In this moneth was put a new Impost upon wine, £3 per Ton, whereat the Merchants, being offended, carryed the greatest part of their wines into Flanders and other parts. So that it is thought it will be taken away againe.

March
The King of France was now enclining unto a treaty with the Protestants, but the report of their taking Clerac, and putting to route of the Earle of Rochfoucault, and the killing of the President of Grenoble by the men of Mompellier, sent thither by the Duke of Dedsigueres, so incensed the king, that they report he is now gone forward to make warre upon them.

25 March 1622
Divers Embassadors were dispatcht away from London. Lord Digby for Spaine, Lord of Doncaster for france, Lord of Chichester to the Emperour, and Sir Richard weston unto the Archduchesse Isabella. Sir John Sucklin, a Papist, is made Secretary of State.

Count Mansfeld, being gotten into the Bishopriks of Spires, Mentz and Colon made great spoile, gotte great booty to pay his souldiers, being 22000 men strong, where he protests he will not cease to permmit all manner of hostility, untill the Palatinate be restored unto the right Lord. And afterwards he increased exceedingly, hath taken into his hands the whole Bishopricke of Spiere saving one Towne. The Duke of Brunswick, also Bishop of Haberstadt, is Come downe with some 10000 men to assist him, and so they fight for the King of Bohemia under the name of his State-holders, who is gone to joyne with Count Mansfeld.

Aprill
In the beginning of this moneth ther came a great Ambassador from the Emperor to our King, his embassage is yet unknowen. His

comming was the cause that the Embassadors appointd to goe to the Emperor and the Low Countreys Archduchesse were staid at home.

The King of France went forward toward Poitou with his army and not far from Nantes came upon some of the Protestants under the conduct of Monsieur de Soubize, unprovided, and having sett upon them and they yeelding themselves to the Kings mercy. The Prince of Conde comming after with another company slew 1500 of the poore Protestants that had laid downe their weapons. But neare about the same time, Monseiur de Rohan fought with the kings forces in Languedoc, under the conduct of Monsieur de Montmorency Admiral of france, overthrew him, slew 4 or 5000 of his men, and hath either slayne or taken the Admiral Prisoner. Upon which reports the king of france is so incensed that he hath taken the Sacrament not to Leave a Protestant in France. From thence he went forward with his army, and planted a seige before Royan, which at last he wan by composition, that the Inhabitants might depart in safety.

At this tyme there was also a shrewd fight Betweene some Hollanders that lay in the River of Bourdeaux, and the Prince of Condé, who being by them feasted abord, planted ordinance in a wood by the shore and shot in among them. Whereupon they shot into the citty and made a great spoille. Which so incensed the cittizens that they massacred all the Hollanders and Protestants that were in it. The men of war got downe the River, though with some Losse. From thence then the king went and tooke in some small townes about Languedoc and by Mony wan Mr de la force to Leave the protestants, and to follow his party, to whome he gave the office of Mareschal.

In the meane time the sicknesse growes very hot in the Kings army. Monsieur de Soubise after his overthrow came in to England in June, and was well Received of the King of England. What assistance he shall have is not yet knowen.

[May]
About this moneth were diverse battailes fought in and about the Palatinate betweene Tilly, the Emperors Generall, and the king of Bohemia and Mansfeld, with diverse successes. But among the rest, Tilly to hinder Brunswicks Joyning with Bohemias king, set

upon him, who retiring two dayes together, lost not in all above 200 men. Presently after he set also upon Brunswicks army, overthrew him, put him to flight, and slew about a thousand, how many I know not.

27 June
Captayne Gould left his band of men and mr Thomas Pelham undertooke it. He chose William Whiteway the younger, his lieutenant.

In this moneth was there a watch appointed in all high wayes through out England, at every crosse way one by day, and two by night perpetually, to give notice, if any tumult should arise for want of trade, as there did of late in Wiltshire and Glocestershire.

July
We had newes that the Grand Signor Osman was strangled, and that his Unkle Mustapha was made Emperor in his place, who is all that is left of the Ottoman Race. He was slayne because he denied to pay the Janizarys their wages in the Polonian warres and told them, they had not don their dutyes.

The 15th hereof in the Morning Thomas Waltham caried away Joane Horsford and maried her at Lidlinch. And the 17th hereof, in the morning at 7 of the Clocke, Mr Denis Bond maried Mrs Luce flea, widow to Mr flea Minister, daughter to Mr William Lawrence of Steepleton, Gentleman.

The 20th hereof we had newes that the Lord Digby was made Earle of Bristol. The Vicount Doncaster, Earle of Kendall. The Lord Cranfield Earle of Middlesex and the Vicont Doncaster a little after made Earle of Carlile.

20 July
At this tyme came newes that the King of Bohemia, and Count Mansfelt wanting provision in the Palatinate, went from thence, Mansfelt into Lorraine, meaning from thence to helpe the Protestants with 25000 men. Their is great watch in the sea costs of Normandy for feare of Soubizes Landing, who is now going for france with 500 voluntaries, after whome a greater number shalbe sent. Which gives the King of france great discontent.

1622

August

In the beginning of this moneth Sir Edward Cooke, and Sir Robert Philips, were delivered out of the Tower.

19th herof was an exceeding great storme, in which diverse ships were cast away, among the rest were 7 ships bound for Rochell at Plimouth, in which were drowned 150 men. The weeke following Mr de Soubize went towards Rochell.

At this tyme the king set out Directions for preachers: to restraine them from meddling with some points.

The former storme did very great spoile unto all maner of corne, so that the last of August Wheate was sold with us for 7s 4d the Busshell.

19th hereof, the day of the great storme, Mansfelt returned out of Lorreyne towards Brabant, having agreed with the States to serve them, and being by the way encountered by Gonzalo de Cordova. After severall and doubtfull bickerings for three dayes, at last they fought a set battaile in Brabant, from 6 in the morning to 3 in the afternoone, wherein Mansfelt lost 2000 men, Gonzalo 3000. Mansfelt took his ordinance and baggage. Brunswick was that day wounded, yet won the field, and rode to the Hague in Gonzalos owne Coach. From thence their army marched unto Breda, to raise the seige from Bergen ap Zome, which had beene long beseiged by Spinola, wherein he hath lost many 1000 men, and won nothing. Brunswicke hath lost his arme.

In france during this tyme, Mr dedigueres turned Papist and was made Constable of france, and laboured to make a peace, but while this was treating of, and that some of the cheife Protestants would have delivered up Montpellier and other Townes unto the King, the Townesmen, understanding it, received them with their Canon and slew as is said in one night 5000, amongst the rest many great men. Rochelle is beseiged also, but to small purpose. 8000 men are before it, and have raised a Mount.

September

In this season was built the common Brewhouse in Dorchester, for the maintenance of the Hospitall.[7]

[47]

30th dicto, were chosen for Baillives
of Dorchester for this yeare.

Undersheriffe.

Mr John Gould, M[erchant].

Mr John Harbin, his eldest son.

Mr Bernard Toope, primus.

Governor of the company of

Constables.

freemen.

John Long: Bookeseller.

Mr John Blachford.

Richard Savidge, Draper.

Assistants to him.

Robert Lawrence.

Robert Coker.

Shooemaker.

James Gould.

Sheriffe.

Thomas Whittell.

Mr John Harbin of Newton.

William Whiteway, junior.

Joseph Whittle was put from his office of Sergeant, and Thomas
Devenish placed in his Roome.

Ships came out of Spaine, about Some twenty Saile, through the
narrow seas, to watch for the Hollanders that tooke some of the
King of Spaines West India fleetes in their way homeward, of
which one was cast away in the Downes, with 140 men and much
treasure.

[October]
Mr de Soubize tooke a Dunkerker going for the Low Countreyes
with £40000 sterling in mony and much other Riches.

October the 10th we had newes of a peace concluded in france betweene the king and the Protestants, upon this condition, that the
Protestants should have Rochell and Mountauban for places of
Security. Mompellier and Nismes and all their other Townes
should be Raised. At this time the king had lost many men, yea
many great men at the seige of Mompellier.

24th hereof Mr Robert Walker was solemnely betrothed to my Sister in Law Mrs Margaret Parkins.

November
We had certaine newes of the concluding of the peace in france, but
it seemes rather to meane onely the towne of Base Languedoc, then
the Protestantes of france in Generall. At this time also we had
great speech of another Parlament that his Majesty meant to call.
Withall we heard 9th dicto the confirmation of the Peace in France.

1622

22 October

The Bishop of Bristoll Dr Searchfield died, in whose roome succeeded Doctor Wright, formerly deane of Welles.

November

After that Mansfelt had raised the Seige of Bergen ap Zome, hee marched up towards Westphalia to punish the Archbishop of Collogne for Assisting Bavaria. The Prince of Orange and Spinola looke one on another.

In this meane time Tilly tooke Heidelberg in the Palatinat, and after that had Manheim yelded up unto him by Sir Horace Veere that was in it, upon very honorable termes: to depart with bag and baggage, colours flying etc. and two pieces of Ordinance. Sir Horace Veer and his Company is Conducted homewards, and so bound for England.

The king of Spaine sent word to the Emperor that if he make not Bavaria restore the Palatinate to the Count Palatin, he himselfe will come and win it for him. A while after at the Diet at Ratisbone the Emperor bestowed the Palatinat with the Electorship upon Maximilian Duke of Bavaria.

26 November

I began my Dutch dictionary taken out of Minsheres ἡγεμὼν ἐις κτλ [guide into etc] ended 9th January 1622.

6 December

This day a quarter of an howre after Nine in the Morning was borne my eldest Son and baptised two daies after by the name of William, astantibus my father, my father in law, and Mrs Joan Gould the widow. I pray god to Blesse him.

The 13th hereof died Mr Oliver Haine, Alderman, in whose place succeeded Mr John Blachford, sworne 3rd January at Sessions.

This winter Corne was very deare, so that Wheate was sold in London for 11s the small bushell, with us for 7s 6d, bar[l]y for 3s 8d and so proportionally after, wheate for 8s barly for 5s.

[49]

1623

4 January 1622/3
There Came certaine newes out of Spaine that the Match was Concluded, and thereupon the King commanded 10 ships to be made ready to fetch the Infanta under the Conduct of the Earle of Rutlande who is to goe Admirall in that Navy.

20 January
This day mr Robert walker was by Mr White maried to my Sister in Law Mrs Margaret Parkins.

30 January
This day about one a clocke in the afternoone this towne tooke on fire in the house of mr John Adin in the higher parish, burnt 27 houses in that parish thereabouts, to the value of £3500 sterling. One man was burnt in William Shepherds house, to wit Edmond Benvenue, who running home, all blacke and deformed by the fire, and being followed by some freinds, they Laboured to stay him to have him drest, was met by mr Cokers man Jaspar Arnold. He thinking him to be some felon, had a pole in his hand, and beate him with it greivously, and strooke him downe. He died within two daies. The Kings Majestie granted for it a Collection over all England.[8]

    This moneth there was much talke of a discovery of the poisoning of Prince Henry deceased, by one Mr Coppinger a servant to the earle of Somersett, but now it is vanished againe, and they say Coppinger is lightheaded.

February
The beginning of february came newes of the discovery of a great treason in the low Countrys against the Prince of Orange, King and Queen of Bohemia, and theirs that were alltogether at the Hage, among which two of old Barnevelts sons ar found guilty, but are fled. Divers of them yet are taken.

The 17th of this moneth Prince Charls, George Marques Bucking-

1623

ham, Baronet Cottington, Endymion Porter, rode post secretly towards Spaine, yet with his Majesties Leave, and arrived safe at Diepe 2 daies after. From whence they went forward, arrived at Paris the friday night, being the 21th of february, and being weary rested there all Satterday, saw the french king, and departed thence on Sonday Morning. And so at length arrived at Madrid, [Prince Charles] having borne the name of Thomas Smith, Sir Cottingtons man, and having beene twice examined in England before he went. In thirteene daies after he arrived in france, he Came to the Spanish Court where he was highly entertained. The king of Spaine to gratify him set open all the prisons, gave him the disposing of all offices that fall during his abode there. The Queene sent him a night gowne and Cabinet valued at 20000 pound. The Marques Buckingham being there, had letters patents sent him to create him Duke of Clarence: My Lord Digby having beene before made Erle of Bristoll and Lord Cranfeld, Earle of Middlesex. Duke of Lennox was made Duke of Richmond.

Aprill 1623
We heard that Count Mansfeild was hardly beset by Gonsalez de Cordova about Embden, and had beene overthrowne, had not the Duke of Brunswicke, that was not far off, come to assist him, and set so furiously upon the Spaniards that they overthrew them. Mansfeld slew Gonsalez with his owne hand. The Spaniards lost 14000 men and Count Mansfeld 8000 men.

17 May
Received of Mr John Parkins my father in Law twelve poundes, ten shillings in full of a legacy due to my wife, given by her Grand-mother Chappelle.

Corne having beene deare all the [blank] begins now somewhat to fall in price, as from 8s to 6s. And the 28th of this moneth, after a long drowth of more then two moneths we had a good showre of Rayne.

The 25th May being Sunday there Landed at Weymouth, the Lord Cary out of Spaine, Lord Chamberlaine to the Prince, with many of the Princes servants. They rodd away presently post to the Court and ten daies after Came over an Extraordinary Embassador from Spaine, but his message is not yet knowne.

[51]

The 30th May about 7 a clocke in the morning died Mrs Gould my
Aunt, wife to mr John Gould Bailiffe, aged about 72 yeares and was
buried the 4th June.

[June]
The 1st June died Mrs Arundell freake of Upway, daughter to Sir
George Trenchard knight.

There was a speech that the Pope Gregory 15th was dead, after
whom Cardinal Barbarino was chosen Pope, and called himselfe
Urban 8th.

This moneth the king of France sent an army into the Low Countreys by the way of Calais, under Mr desdigueres Constable of France,
but most men thinke it is to Joine with Count Mansfelt to recover
the Valtellin from the king of Spaine.

This moneth there arrived at London a great Embassador out of
Spaine, sometimes Viceroy of Naples, and presently after him,
came two great men English also out of Spaine. At the same time
there was a stir betwixt the Noblemen bound for Spaine in the
Navy, for they troubling the Master and Mariners in their praiers,
were by them ducked at Mayne yard, and amongst the Rest, the Lord
Morley. Whereupon the king dismissed the Mariners, onely sent one
ship for Spaine, and one into Scotland to free a Dunkirker. But
within a moneth after the said ships had order againe to goe for
Spaine.

The Prince of Orange was wounded by a villain, but is in way of
recovery. The Hollanders have made peace with the Pirats of Al-
gier, and betweene them have taken 6 Brasill men and divided the
Spoile ⅔ for Holland.

July
The 17th of this moneth, the Assises were held at Dorchester by Sir
Lawrence Tanfield Lord cheife Baron and Sir Richard Hutton.
There was executed but one man.

In this moneth, the french king sent a fleete of ships to blocke up
Rochell by sea, where Mr De Guise is expected also with 20 Gallies
from Bourdeaux. But within a while they all went away againe, and
ther is like to be peace all this yeare. Som thinke, ther was some
treason entended against Rochell but prevented.

The 31th hereof, halfe an howre after 9 in the evening, there fell a great storme of haile, with thunder and lightning. The haile was as big as a beane, and after followed a wet harvest.

August

This moneth the kings Majesty came in Progress to Sarum and Cranborne. At Sarum he held a Solemne feast 4 daies Together.

The beginning of this moneth we had newes of a great overthrow given by the Duke of Brunswicke unto Tilly, the Emperors Lieutenant, and that Brunswicke marched from thence towards Bavaria, having slaine 7000 of the Emperors souldiers in the Battell. But this was countermanded, and the quite Contrary reported.

The 2nd of this moneth Henry St George Richmond, Sargeant at armes and Sampson Lennard Blewmantle Pursevant, Came in the Heralds visitation being 48 yeares since the last visitation, and tooke accompt of all the Armes that were borne in the Country. This somer they went over Dorset, Somerset, Wiltes, and Hamshire, having beene the sommer before in Devon and Cornwall. They staid in Dorchester 4 daies and went hence the 7th dicto to Sherborne and thence for Somersett.

The 21th of this moneth about noone died Mr Tobiah Sanford Physition of this Towne, and was buried the next day, a man of very excellent skill in the English and Latine tongues.

The 25th of this moneth, the kings ships arrived in Portland in their voiage for Spaine, to bring home the Prince and his Lady; they reportd that the Prince was marryed the 24th dicto and was to com from Madrid 4 daies after, and at the end of twenty days to be at the Seas side, to take shipping. The Earle of Rutland is Generall of the fleete, with him are diverse Lords. They departed from Weymouth the next day about midnight. The Prince Roiall being Admirall is a vessell of wonderfull bignes, strength, and beauty.

This somer died Pope Gregory the 15th and in his place was chosen Cardinal Barbarino a Florentine, who named himselfe Urban the eighth, or as some say, Clement the 9th, but in fine it was Urbane the 8.

4 September

This day we went for London and returned 23 daies after, having staid in London 16 daies. During our abode there, mr Edward Prichard died. There came newes of the Prince his arrivall at Portesmouth, and ballads were made of it, but it prooved false, the balladsingers were sent to prison. While we were there, a man ready to be buryed revived and lived halfe a day. About this autumne the younge Dutchesse of Buckingham being daughter to a great Papist, turned a very sound Protestant, and Dr white gave Mr fisher a Jesuite a foule overthrow in a disputacion.

1 October

This day I rode for Exon about the overthrowinge a sentence given by the counsell of State at Paris to seaze upon £10000 sterling of English goods, if before the 16th March next, there were not satisfaction made to those french men that Mannering robd at Sea.

On the way I heard that the Earle of Montgomery was made Master of the horse, the office having belonged formerly to the Duke of Buckingham. [*This entry has been crossed through.*]

6 October

This day were chosen for Dorchester

Bailiffes.	Assistants.
Mr William Jolliffe 2.	John Long.
Mr Dionis Bond 1.	Matthew Butler.
Constables.	John Condit.
Richard Savidge, Draper.	Joseph Underwood.
Morgan Hayne, Mercer.	Sheriffe of Dorset.
Edward Dashwood, Clothier.	Mr Arthur Radford, prickt by
Governor.	the prince.
Joseph Paty Clothier.	Under sheriffe.
	John Champneyes 2d.

5 October

This day being Sunday, the Prince with the Duke of Buckingham and others arrived at Portesmouth at two of the clocke at afternoone, and rode to London the next day. At his Coming home was great joy. The great pieces were shott of twice in Dorchester. The match was not concluded of, but there came after certeyn ambass[adors] to treate farther of it.

Dr Wright our new Bishop kept his visitacion here this yeare in September. Mr Cheeke acted two comedies at the sheere hall for his coming, by his schollers.

26 October
This day being Sonday, about 5 a clocke in the Evening about 300 papists being assembld at Hunsdon howse in Blackfriars at London, in a faire [chambre], while the Jesuit was in his exhortacons, and in the midst of ther devotion the loft fell downe, and bare downe another loft so that were slaine about 100 persons amongst which were many great persons, whose bodies are stollen away by their freinds. The meaner sort were buried there outright, without Masse or Matins.

10 November
Alderman Cockins house was burnt in London with 3 more in Broadstreete. Sir William Cocking lost above £14000 sterling in goods and Stuffe.

15 November
This day about 10 a clocke at night Squire Williams stabd the Tapster of the George to the heart and killd him. Whereupon he fled into Holland, and from thence to france, where he lived at Caen. Some 8 moneths after he returned, having a pardon for £1500.

[*Here follows a cancelled passage which is illegible.*]

The beginning of this moneth ther came in at Weymouth a Polacra, in which 11 Christians of diverse nacions slew 9 Turks that were ther masters, and brought home alive 16 more.

The 16th of this moneth stilo novo there was a great uprore in Roan in france, by meanes of a tax the King meant to lay upon the commonalty. Which Continued 2 daies and in which divers rich men had their houses rifled. 6 or 7 men were killd, and abo[ve].

The 12th hereof Alderman Cockin had his house burnt in Broadstret in London, wherein he lost £14000. There were 3 other houses burnt also.
Before this tyme, in steed [of] the Duke de luynes Constable of

France, the King of france had another favorite, one Mr de Puisieulx, an advocates sonne, and sometimes secretary of State. He is now made Duke of Chartres.

16 December
This day about 7 a clocke at night the new Brewhouse killne was on fire and the yeast quite burnt. At this tyme for the space of 10 daies we had a most violent frost. About this tyme also, there began to be a speech of a Parliament; but nothing yet certeinely knowne. The Spanish match also is uncerteinly reported of.

The 15 hereof, Sir Walter Erle, Governour of the New England plantacion, came hither to advize with the rest of the planters about the ordering the busynesse. A share is £5 a yeare to be paid yearly for 5 yeares, and then shalbe made a distribution of the proffits. I have subscribed to be one Share. We had newes of a great over-throw given by Bethlem Gabor to the Emperour, who fled and left Austria for a prey.

December
The day of our Princes marriage being appointd in Spaine, there arrived a post from England, to signify that the prince would not have the Lady, unless the Palatinate were presently surrendred, at which the king of Spaine grew very angry. About this time also was discovered a conspiracy in London, of certeyn priests against our King, prince, and the rest of his issue.

The Spaniards made an attempt on Eysendick, but failed by the overgreat shortness of the bridge they brought to pass the mote that environed the Towne.

The 26th hereof died mr John Spicer alderman, having beene many yeares in decay of his understanding. In his roome was chosen in the next Sessions Mr James Gould, Merchant, at the age of 30.

1624

January 1623/4

About the beginning of this moneth the Earle of Oxford was sett at liberty, having beene 2 yeares and ½ in the Tower, about some words he spake at the Court. Since his enlargement he maried Diana Cecill daughter to the Earle of Exceter. At this time, there was a report that Sir Edward Cooke, and Sir Robert Philips, should be sent commissioners into Ireland. As also that the Baron of Kensington should goe for france to negotiat a match betweene the Prince, and the king of France his Sister, the Lady Henriette Marie, there being now an ambassador arrived out of france to the same purpose.

The 11th hereof died Mr Rogers Esquire that married the eldest daughter of Sir John Strangeways, he died at Abbotsbury of the small pockes, aged about 18 yeares, and was buried 4 daies after at Blandford.

About this time there was a great overflowing of waters in Holand by which many parrishes were drowned.

Memorandum

That the last yeare Mustapha the Grand Signor, who had deposed and put to death his Nephew Osman, was now agayne deposed by the bassa of Cairo, and Amurath 4 yonger brother to Osman set in the Othoman throne. Wherupon arose great stirs in Natolia, so that the [v]isir bassa was faine to recall those souldiers that wer gone to assist Bethlem Gabor.

2 February

The Parlement being to begin the 12th hereof, this day were chosen knights for the Shire. Sir John Strangewaies. Sir George Horsey.

The 26th January were chosen
Burgesses for dorchester.
    Mr William Whiteway Senior.
    Mr Richard Bushrod.

[57]

For Weymouth and Melcombe
  Regis.
Burgesses.
  Mr Matthew Pitt.
  Mr Thomas Giere.
Gentlemen.
  Mr John Freake.
  Mr Pines son.
For Bridport.
  Mr Musten.
  Mr Robert Browne.
For Poole.
  Sir Walter Earle.
  Mr Edward Pitt, son to
    Sir William Pitt.
For Shaftesbury.
  Mr Thoroughgood.
  Secretary to E [?Prin].
  Mr Whitaker, a Barrister.
For Corffe.
  Sir Francis Netherson.
  Sir Robert Osborne, knight.

For Wareham.
  Sir William Pitt.
  Mr John Trenchard.
Knights of Somersetshire.
  Sir Robert Philips.
  Mr Symmes of Chard.
Of Devonshire.
  Sir William Strode.
  Mr John Drake.
Of Wiltshire.
  Edward Hungerford,
  Esquire.
  Sir John St. John.
Of Hamshire.
  Sir Robert Oxenbridge.
  Sir Daniel Norton.
Burgesses of Exon.
  Mr Ducke, Recorder.
  Mr John Prowse.
of Lyme.
  Mr Christopher Earle.
  Mr Hazard, Courtier.

At the choosing of knights for Dorsett the 2nd february Sir
Nathaniel napper stood for the place, being promised that Sir
George Horsey should not stand, and thereupon leaving most of
his freeholders behind. The cry was very confusd, so that the
sheriffe sware the freeholders that came to give their voices and Sir
Nathaniel Napper lost it by 70 voices. But the Contrary faction had
such a blott cast upon them for their double dealing that they will
not easily wipe it of.

The end of January, and beginning of this moneth, wee had extreame frost, and much snow, so that many died of cold upon the
high wayes. The River Thames was frozen over.
    This tyme was ther £300 collected among the french marchants
of the wholle Westerne parts, to be paid Mr Daniel Harvey, for the
overthrowing an Edict granted in france against the goods of English marchants, for the piracies of captaine Mannering. Of this
some Dorchester paid £30, Melcombe 20, Hampton 30.

1624

[Here a cancelled entry dated 14th, apparently in Italian but illegible.]

All this winter the small pockes were very thicke in this Towne of which many children died, and some elder people.

At this tyme a Popish Lawyer about London was censured at the Star chamber for saying that king henry 8 did piss the Protestant relligion out of his codpiece, to have his eares cut of, his nose slit, his forehed marked with B. for blasphemy, whipt about London, and fined £12000 to the king.

12 February
The Parlement being summoned for this day was adjourned untill the 16th because the Earle of Bristoll was not yet come out of Spaine. When the 16th day Monday was come, and all things preparing, Lewys duke of Richmond and Lennox, Lord high Steward of England, was found dead in his bed about 9 a clocke, having never complained but an howre before, that his head did ake. Upon that occasion the Parlament was againe adjourned to the 19th dicto and the Earle of Pembroke made Lord high Steward, to sweare the rest of the Parlement menne. That day being Thursday the king rode to Parliament in a Stately chariot, drawne with 6 blacke genetts, accompanied with the Prince and all the Nobility. Where his Majesty declared his mind in a most gratious speech, the substance whereof was, that he had called them together, to treate about the recovery of the Palatinate and their proceeding in the Spanish match. Three daies after, they presented unto the king, Sir Thomas Crew to be their speaker, who made an excellent speech unto the higher howse, and was excellently answered by the Lord keeper.

The 24th hereof the Prince with the Duke of Buckingham declared unto both the houses assembled in the Painted chamber, all letters and passages of the Spanish match, and of the Prince his Journey into spaine, with great dislike of their enterteinment there, and of the proceedings of the Spaniards. Whereupon a while after at Whitehall the Prince and both houses declared their meaning to treat no longer with the king of Spaine about the match and Palatinate. Upon this the Spanish Embassador demands of the king of England the Duke of Buckingams head, for dishonouring his master, as he affirmed in his relation. The matter being

[59]

referred to the houses, they quitted and commended my Lord Duke [*blank*]. To both houses was administred the oath of allegiance, which 5 of the Nobility Refused, and forsook the house, as Lord Winsor, Lord Mordant, Lord Vaux, Lord Morley, Lord montague.

The end of this moneth Spinola entred into Holland over the Ice, but the States souldiers brake the Ice behind him, so that in his returne he lost 2000 men and among them 5 or 600 horse.

8 March
Sir Arthur Smitheyes came to this Towne to dwell, with his houshold.

The 5th of this moneth, both the houses of Parliament having determined to make war upon the Spaniards for the Palatinat, sent a Subcommittee to the king to Theobalds, to crave his approbation. He thanked them for their care and readynes, told them that he was poore, and that they must open their purses aswell as their harts, but that since the Parlement beganne, he had had fairer treaty with the Spanish and upon better termes. In conclusion he proposed unto them divers difficulties to be discussed, and promised upon their answere to resolve upon peace or warre. To this they answered by a comittee sent to the king at whitehall the 14th hereof, the archbishop of Canterbury delivering the messages. That if his Majesty would breake of the Treatys with Spaine, their lives and estates should be at his service. Upon this his Majesty demanded of them 5 subsidies and 2 fifteenes to each subsidy for the warres, and for his owne debts one subsidy and 2 fifteenes every yeare while he lived. The howses deliberating upon this, the 20th dicto resolved to give his Majesty for the warres 3 subsidies and 6 fifteenes, to be paid within a yeare after he should declare himselfe to have broken of the treatys with Spaine, of the match and the Palatinate, with condition that this be made a Session of Parliament. Which offer of theirs his Majesty accepted graciously and brake of both Treaties. So the Parliament was adjourned from the 25th March to the 1 of Aprill.

27 March 1624
This day was buryed the Lady Magdelene Napper, who died 4 daies before, widdow to Sir Robert Napper, knight.

31th dicto were the Comittes chosen for the new England busynesse at the free schole, Sir Walter Erle Governor, Mr Humphreys Esquire Treasurer.

Sir Richard Strode.	Mr Edward Clarke.
Sir Arthur Smitheys.	Mr John Hill.
Mr John Browne.	Mr William Derby.
Doctor Bradish.	Mr James Gould.
Mr John keate.	William Whiteway, junior.
Mr Giles Greene.	Mr Henry Maniford.

The 27th of this moneth died The earle of Dorset, my Lord Mordant also: diverse noblemen were sicke. The earle of Oxford broke his arme at Tilt.

The king of france supplied the Hollanders with 600000 crownes and Mansfelt is to be made Mareshal of france and to serve against the Spaniards.

1 Aprill
The Duke of Buckingham, and my Lord Treasurer are fallen out, the Prince takes the Dukes part, and is one of the Comittes to heare the cause. Shortly after divers accusations were laid in and prooved against the said Lord Tresurer, as for defrauding his Majesty, in the farme of grocery of about 4000 or £5000 per annum, of Continuing the merke per Ton upon wynes, without the kings leave, for taking of bribes, and abusing the Court of wards of which he was master, but especially for not supplying the powder for the kings Store in the Tower, so that there is great want of it through the wholle Land. He was censured the 13th May to pay £50000 to the king, to bee deprived of all his offices, and to ly in the Tower during his Majesties pleasure, and made incapable of any office or place in parlement.

5 Aprill
Two men were found Landed at Lullworth, a Spaniard and an Englishman with many letteres to divers Papists, they were apprehended and by Sir George Trenchard, and Sir Edward Lawrence sent to London.

The 16th hereof Count Mansfelt Came to London, where he was honorably received by the Court, lodged in St James. Having spoken with his Majesty about some important busyness, he departed for france the 26th of this moneth.

Mr Matthew Pitt of weymouth died in London the 18th Aprill and was buryed there by night two daies after. In his place was chosen the 10th May Sir Thomas Middleton Junior of London.

The 24th hereof the Spanish Embassador told the king of England that it wer good for him to looke to himself for the Prince, duke of Buckingham, with the Parlement, had conspired to depose him and set the Crowne on the Princes head. Which being found false, the king commanded the Lord Maior of London to apprehend and examine all English men that frequented the Embassadors house.

The end of this moneth my Lord Digby, Earle of Bristoll, came home out of his long Embassage in Spaine. He was brought from Gravesend to London in the kings barge the 5th May and shortly after was confined to his house. The Countesse landed at Weymouth and past through this towne 10 daies before.

8 May
This day, proclamation was made in London, that all Jesuits, priests, and Seminarys should depart out of this Land before the 14th June next, upon pain of the Severest Censure of the Lawes.

The 28th Aprill this yeare Cousin James Gould was married to his wife at Bloxworth, and the next day brought her home. La Dote vi si era di cinquecento lire. [*There was a dowry of five hundred pounds.*]

29 May
The Parliament sate untill this day and then adjourned it to the 2nd of November. In this Session were granted 3 subsidies to the assistance of the low Countrys, to securing of Ireland, the setting out of the Navy Royall and safety of our coasts. To be put into the hands of 8 Treasurers of London, and to be disposed of by the Counsell of war onely. The king grantd his generall Pardon as accustomed. He past a great many good Lawes, refused to pass the bill for the Sabbath. He blamed the house for taking away the Patents they had viewed, and willed them to restore them. And the speech is that 6000 men are shortly to goe to the Low Countrys under the Earle of Southampton, and other noblemen.

1624

[Here a cancelled entry mainly, it appears, in Italian but illegible.]

This Somer the common Jaile in Dorchester in the east streete was finished.

1 June
This day the Earle of Middelsex, committed to the Tower by the Parliament as abovesaid, was by the king sett at liberty, and sworne one of the Gentlemen of his Majesties Bedchamber.

The Duke of Buckingham having beene dangerously sicke of Late, and for that purpose remooved from London to Newhall in Essex, recovered and came to the Court againe. The king this somer went his progress Northward. The Earle of Bristoll desires to be heard, and give account of his Embassage, but Cannot obtyne it.

The king denyed the Spanish Embassador audience, and appoints a merchant ship to carry him home.

The Prince this somer, went the Progress with the king, and Lay every night in the same howse.

There was great speech at this time of the marriage of the Prince with the king of france his Sister. Sir Henry Rich, Baron of Kensington, went Embassador to Paris about this busynes, as is it supposed.

At this tyme came home the king of Spains West India fleet, with a great deale of treasure.

1 July
This day began the Assises here, held by Sir Lawrence Tanfield, and Sir Richard Hutton. There were 8 men executed.

At this tyme the Drum went about London to gather 6000 voluntarys to serve against the Spaniards, but after it was proclaymed to Serve the States under the Earle of Oxford, my Lord Willoughby, Colonel Veer and Colonel Cecill and they are to enter into pay presently. Ther was much sute about Captains places and other officers. In the beginning of August they went over with som 10000. At this tyme we had newes that the king of Sweden had raisd an army of 40000 men and 70 ships, under the pretence of going against Poland, and presently turned himself against Denmarke, threatning that if the king did not subscribe to such artecls, as he proposed within 3 daies, he would overrunne his Countrey.

[63]

The 5th July the subsidy was assessd in Dorchester together with the fifteenth. The subsidy amounted to about some £24 in this Towne, a ¹⁄₁₅ unto som 6 pound.

The 11th hereof about ½ an houre after 6 a clocke in the evening being Sunday, my 2nd daughter was borne and baptised by mr Clarke the 18th dicto being Sunday. The godfather was mr Joseph Paty my Unkle. Godmothers, mrs Margaret Walker my Sister, and my Cousin mrs Margery Gould, by whom she was called Margaret.

This Somer was very dry and so continued to the beginning of September and wheat grew worth 6s.

August
The beginning of this moneth, Esme Lord Aubigny, Duke of Winsore, younger brother to the Late Duke of Richmond, died.

Thend of this moneth we had news that the Hollanders had taken de todos Santos Baye a place of great importance in Brasil from the Spaniards, and that another fleet of them in the South sea had Joyned with the Chilois against the Spaniard, had taken their Governors son, the Archbishop, and 250 brass peices.

At this very tyme Spinola laid seige to Breda where to shew the Prince of Poland sport, he assaulted the citty but was bravely repulsed with the loss of 500 of his best men.

1 September
Sir Robert Meller knight died at the Bath and was buryed at Came at Midnight, mr Guy preaching.

7th of this moneth 6 houses were burnt at Poole about midnight, and a day before, one house at Blandford.

At this tyme the Prince of Poland past through flanders into Spaine to woe the Spanish Lady.

25 September
John Ward was bound Apprentice unto my father and my selfe for 9 yeares from this day.

About this time Count Mansfelt returned out of france to London and in the beginning of October, returned againe for france. It is said, he shall have 15000 men follow him out of England.

September 26th Cousin James Gould the younger was marryed at Exon to Mr Marshalls daughter.

At the towne Sessions Patroclus Cooke was put out of his office of Sargeant, for some words spoken against my Lord cheif Baron and John Condit put in his place.

2 October

This night there was an extraordinary storme of wynd and rayne, which blew downe many houses, overthrew many great trees, cast away many ships in all ports, amongst the rest 4 at Melcombe in the hole, of which one was mr Pits, one mr Royes and 2 french men. There were 11 french men drownd in the same.

4 October
The day were chosen Bailiffes for Dorchester.

		Assistants.
Mr John Parkins 4.	Bailifs.	Simon Haselbury.
Mr John Hill 1.		Henry Sims.
Constables.		Richard Savidge.
Edward Dashwood, Clothier.		Matthew Buttler.
Henry Derby, mercer.		Sherife of Dorsett.
Joseph Underwood, Grocer.		Mr Banfill Chaffin, Esquire.
Governour.		Undersherife.
William Whiteway thyounger.		Mr William Goldesney.

At this tyme Sir James Lee, Lord cheif Justice, was made Lord Treasurer and Sir Randall Crue was made Lord cheife Justice in his place. The Prince fell from his horse in hunting, and was sorely hurt. The king lay Sicke of the Goute at Newmarket.

2 November
The Parliament that was adjourned unto this day, was now put of to the 4th of february next and from thence to the 24th of the same moneth.

5 November
The seige of Breda continued still, the towne being environed round by Spinola. The Prince of Orange with our English and 30000 Lay encamped close without him, but about this tyme re-mooved to intercept his Vittailes. In the meane time Count Mansfeld came this day the 3rd time into England, and his demands

were gratiously answered and forthwith 12000 men levied for him in England, 10000 in Scotland. In our towne were taken up 14 lusty fellows 19th dicto.

The ship in which Count Mansfeld came over was cast away, being our kings ship. 160 men drowned and among them 60 of his traine, many great Commanders among them.

At the seige abovenamed the Earle of Southampton, and his sonne and heire both died, one the wensday, the other the Thursday. The Earle of Oxford was shot, but is like to recover. The Prince of Orange was caried sicke out of the army, all not without suspition.

The 16th dicto we had newes that the Prince his match with france was concluded. At the same time, the Duke of Buckingham was Created Prince of Tiperary, a place in Ireland.

21 November
This day the king commanded Bonfires, ringing of bells, discharging of Ordinance at London for the conclusion of the french match. The Prince of Tiperary goes to fetch her very shortly. The prince borrowed £35000 of the Citty of London to furnish himself against his maridge.

The end of this moneth falling on extraordinary wett weather, Spinolas camp was so overflowen, that he remooved a league further of from the Towne, and by that meanes the Prince of Orange conveyed in provision for 6 moneths more. But yet the seige continued strongly maintained with about 50 or 60000 men.

3 December
The Prince of Joinville came embassador out of France to conclude the match, and went to Cambridge to the king, where he was feasted.

The Duke of Arschot at Brussels, persuading the raising the seige of Breda, was the next night slayne in his bed.

Voluntarys were at this time taken up in London to serve on horsebacke under Count Mansfelt. The Earle of Lincolne was to leade them. The 15 and 20th of this moneth the 12000 souldiers marched towards dover where count Mansfeld attended them to transport them over to Calais and to Joyne with the french forces which are taken up in great abundance in france.

[66]

20th dicto my Cousin P. Middelton took 6d of me, to pay me 5s next tyme I can proove that he drinks tabacco. Was released 19th January.

	£
paid my wife in part this day	10
more the 31th december	10
more the 1 January	05
more the 10th dicto	03
more the 26th dicto	05
5th february	03
March 4	5

24th December the old Count Thurne, and Duke of Brunswick came to London, and were Royally enterteynd. The Duke of Brunswick was made knight of the Garter, and departed 3 January from London.

About this tyme died Sir John Ryves, knight. This winter the king of france by the Marquis of Coeuvres, his general, recoverd the greatest part of the Valtelline, out of the hand of the Spaniards. He levyed also 2000 horse and 7000 foote to meet Count Mansfelt at Calais, wher was expected likewise, many souldiers from Denmark, and 10000 from the German Princes.

1625

1 January 1624/5

The Earle of Lincolne went a Colonell under Count Mansfelt. So did Captain Burrows, Sir Andrew Gray, Sir Nathaniel Rich, the Vicont Doncaster and [blank] being 6 in all. These forces being shipt about the midle of this moneth, tooke their course for the river of Antwerpe where they arrived about the 20th. The seige of Breda still contynuing very strong.

21th dicto Mr Nicholas Vawter was remooved from his place of Capitall Burgess in regard of his absence, and William Whiteway the younger chosen in his place.

Ther was at this tyme great rumors of troubls in france. The Duke of Vendosm was said to be in armes and the Count Soissons challengeth the Princess that was promised to Prince Charls, as having a promise of her made him by Henry the 4th. Soubise seized upon 6 of the french kings ships. The Protestants apprehended some great danger. The king of france his Treasure was said to be robd, whereupon he made a generall stay of all shipping in his dominions, which stay was againe renewed by the Counsell after the death of king James.

16 February

The Parliament that was adjourned to this day, was againe by proclamation adjourned unto the 15th March.

The 3rd hereof mr George Bull was betrothed unto my Sister in Law Elizabeth Parkins.

Captaine Thomas Hayne left his band of men and Maximilian Mohun succeeded him in that place. He held not and so Captain Gould had it.

About Christmas this winter the Archbishop of Spalata, being imprisoned for an Heretike in Rome, died in prison, and was a little after Condemned to have his body burnt.

About the beginning of february, there was a treason descoverd in france against the person of the french king, plotted by priests and Jesuits. Some of the Priestes were hangd at Roan, and some of the Jesuits are now in hold.

10th dicto. We had no cold all this winter, untill this day. Then the frost began and Contynued till the 24th of the same moneth.

13th dicto Mr Robert Coker Esquire died Suddenly at church at Evening Praier.

2 March
Count Mansfelt shipt his army on the end of January and went for the low Countrys, where he is yet remaining. The french force are going to meete him. The king of England lends the french 5 ships to helpe to transport them.

This day and 28th february the Assises were held here by Justice Hutton. My Lord cheife Baron was upon the Commission, but was so sicke that he came not. He went to Westminster the 3 last days of the Terme, that he might not be left out of the Comission. 8 persons were executd, among them one for clipping of silver.

March 4th Captain Crouch was buryd in dorchester with military Pompe.

The beginning of this moneth the state of busynesse began to alter at our Court. The french match was at a stand. The french propounded very unreasonable demands. The Spaniards offered againe to restore the Palatinat, and Gondemar is coming into England to treate with the king. Whereupon Count Mansfelt was commanded not to meddle with any of the king of Spains dominions; no not so much as to releive Breda, though he were now in the low Countrys and Joyned with the french. Besides, the marquis Hamilton died at this tyme, and some 10 daies before him Viscount Grandison, not without suspicion. Thearle of Pembroke also and marquis Hameltons sonne are very sicke.

15 March
The parlement was againe prorogued unto the 20th of Aprill next.

At this time, Sir francis Aishly, knight sergeant at Law, was made the kings sergeant.

[69]

27 March 1625

This day about 3 a clocke in the morning died at Theobalds, our Soveraigne Lord James, king of great Britain, france and Ireland: having rayned 22 years and 3 daies. He died of a burning feaver. The same morning his onely sonne Prince Charles was proclaymed at Theobalds, and in the afternoone at London, by the Name of Charles by the grace of god, king of great Britain, france and Ireland, defender of the faith etc. We heard of it at dorchester 48 hours after his death, and proclaymed him by the Town clarke the 30th dicto after supper. The magistrates assisting.

The Duke of Buckinghams sumptuous journey for france is hindred by the kings death.

His majesty upon his deathbed recommended unto the Prince, the Earles of Pembroke and Montgomery as his best servants and charged him never to suffer a toleration of Popery in England. He made a worthy confession of his faith, and gave great testimonys of devotion and piety. The same day in the afternoone the Lord Maior, Lord Keeper, and divers other noble men, published a declaration, by which they proclaimed King charles and the next day the said King charls Sent forth a proclamacion from St James, to continue all men in the offices they enjoyed during king James his life.

Within 2 daies his majesty sware to himselfe all the old privy Counsell except Sir George Calvert who was refused because he would not take the oath of allegiance, and in his place Sir Humphrey May was chosen who was Chanceller of the dutchy of Lancaster.

4 Aprill

This day the kings James his body was brought from Theobalds unto the Tower of London in Pompe.

The beginning of this moneth there came out a new Summons for a new Parliament. The former by king James, his death quite dissolved.

14 Aprill

This day the house below the Schoole was made over into the hands of mr William derby and mine, for ever and The close that was Mr Haines, to mr Dionis Bond and Mr William Derby, to the use of the free schoole.

1625

The beginning of this moneth, Spinola Lying at the seige of Breda lost a great quantity of vitails and provision by fire, which some say was done by treachery. Count Mansfelt, Brunswic and Grave Henric his brother being extreame sicke, resolved to take the field the 20th Aprill with 70000 foote and 2000 horse.

The french kings forces under the Marquis de Coeure, having taken in all the Valtelline, marched towards Geneva, and laid Seige unto it. The king of Spaine hereupon resolved to goe into Millain himselfe.

This spring there was a very great fleet prepared in England, begun by King James, and after by King Charles, of 140 saile, mariners prest all over england, 250 in Dorsettshire.

The new Parliament being summoned to begin at Westminster upon the 17th day of May, the knights for Dorsett were chosen in Dorchester with great concurse of people. Sir Walter Earle. Sir Nathaniel Napper.

Burgesses for Dorchester.
  Sir francis Aishley.
  William Whiteway the elder.
Burgesses for Melcombe.
  Sir John Strangeways.
  Bernard Michell.
Burgesses for Weymouth.
  Sir Thomas Middelton Junior.
  Arthur Pine Esquire.
Burgesses for Bridport.
  Sir John Strode.
  John Browne Esquire.

Burgesses for Wareham.
  Sir William Pit.
  John Trenchard Esquire.
Burgesses for Poole.
  Sir John Cuper.
  John Pine Esquire.
Burgesses for Corffe.
  Sir francis Nethersol.
  Sir Peter Osborne.
Burgesses for Shaftesbury.
  John Thoroughgood.
  William Whitaker.
Burgesses for Lime.
  John Drake, Esquire.
  John Paramore, Esquire.

About this tym died Maurice Prince of Orange, Generall of the armies of the low Countreys, to whome succeeded his brother Henry frederic.

1 May
This day king Charles was maried to the Lady Mary of france at Paris by proxy made unto the Duke de Chevreuse. Where after

much Contestation about our kings title of king of france, at last about 10 a clock at night it was finished.

This Spring the Sickeness began to spread itselfe in London.

King James was buried with great State upon the 7th May. King Charles went cheife mourner after the Chariot. There were about 80000 Mourners.

The 10th of this moneth died Sir John Fitzjames. Sir George Trenchard was remooved from being Deputy lieutenant, and Sir Nathaniel Napper had it confirmed unto him, and in steed of Sir John Strangwayes came Sir walter Earle.

The Royall Navy went forward apace this moneth consisting of 140 Saile, with which were to Joyn 100 Saile of Flemings, besides Danes and frenchmen. There came a presse for 10000 men to goe to Plymouth to meet this fleete of which 250 were taken up in this shire, and 10 in this towne, by Mr Hastings, and Sir John Browne.

17 May
The Parliament was adjourned unto the 31th hereof, and from thence to the 13th June, being Trinity Monday.

The 16th hereof Sir Horace Vere made an attempt to releive Breda but being repulsed, came away with the loss of 150 English men, which led the Vantgard, amongst them 3 or 4 captayns, and the Earle of oxfords Ensigne was slaine at my Lords feet, who valiantly recovered his colours from his enemys with his owne hand. Whereupon they of the Towne, seing no hope of releif, yeelded up the Towne to Spinola upon very honourable composition, and had it well performed upon the 24th day of May having held out neare eleven moneths.

The 31th hereof king Charles rod towards Canterbury to meete the queene, who arrived at dover the 12th June, at the evening. And so both king and queene came both to whitehall upon the 16th of the same June moneth, being Thursday.

5 June
This day at 11 a clocke at night, god took unto his mercy, my eldest daughter Mary, being fower yeares old within 6 or 7 daies.

13 June

The Parliament adjourned to this day, was againe adjourned by my Lord keeper unto the 18th day being Saterday and then the king came thither, and made a short speech unto the Parliament. The substance whereof was To signify unto them, that whereas upon their advise he had beene a meanes to set forward king James his father into so great a work as this present warre, they would consider his occasions for mony, and bee ready to open ther purses to him. And then my Lord keeper, by the kings command, uttered the sam things more amply.

The 19th hereof, the Earle of Oxford died at the Hague, of a bruise that he received at the seige of Breda, but som think his death was hastened by Poison. He had fallen out with Grave Henrick, and calld him little better then traitor for not seconding the English with his Dutch forces in that attempt upon Spinolas trenches. And Count Henric himselfe begins to be distasted by the States, being himselfe an Arminian.

6 July

This day my Sister Elisabeth Parkins was married privatly unto mr George Bull of wells who carried her thither upon the 11th day of the same moneth.

10 July

This day being Sonday, francis Sanders was taken by french Pirats Laden with kerses, of which they took some, and let the rest goe. The losses were:

	£
To mr John Parkins about	700
To mr Blachford about	350
To mr whiteway about	150
To mr Waltham about	400
	1600

Some others had losses in it also, but of no great value.

The Parliament this Session gave the king 2 Subsidies. The king caused a fast to be proclaymed, to be kept every wensday, during this Sickeness, which was now so great, that there died in London

[73]

1740 in a weeke. This fast was first celebrated with us upon the 20th July, and the [*blank*] of the same moneth, the parliament was adjourned to the 1 of August to be kept at Oxford.

The 21th July our Assises began, held by Justice Hutton alone. Sir John Walter Lord cheife Baron was upon the commission, but came not in regard of the Parliament.

The 11th of this moneth Sir James Hussey Chanceller of Dorsett died suddenly at Oxford and Mr Jones succeeded him in his place.

August
This day the Parliament met and sate in the new Schooles at oxon. Where the king, requiring of him more mony to supply his wants, they absolutely refused, saying that they would not leave such a president to posterity, to give 2 subsidys at Westminster, and then to be called at Oxford for more presently. Upon this the Parliament was dissolved, with great dislike of both sides, the 12th of the same moneth.

The 18th hereof the Sickeness was at the heigth in London, for that week there died 5205 in London and libertys and in westminster and Stepney neare 4000 but afterwards it began to decrease in London. It was dispersed into divers quarters of this kingdome, as to Oxford, Exeter, Winchester, Bath, and all the townes about London, Reading, Abington, Southampton, the Isle of wight. In Dorsettshire are dead 1 at Sherborn, 3 at Moreton. Yeatminster is infected, Martock, Bridgewater. It raigned long and greivously at Exeter all the winter.

This somer the king and queene came from Oxford to Beaulieu and from thence purpose to remoove to Wilton. And upon the 12th September Lay at Bruton, next night at mr Pawlets at Hinton in his Journey to Plimouth to see the Navy.

31 August
This day Sir Edward Cecill, Lord Generall, Lay in Dorchester, riding to Plimouth. And upon the 11th September the Earle of Arundel past through the Towne, to meet the king at Plimouth, who went by the way of Bruton, and Lay there and at mr Pawlets of Hinton, and liked his entertainment so well, that he Lay there also in his

[74]

returne to Wilton the 28th September. The Earle of Arundel returned by dorchester 26th dicto.

Spinola marched up towards Dunkerk with a great army, which put both England and France in fear. The french king fortified Calice, and king Charles sent the Earle of warwick with forces to gard the coast of Kent etc.

September
While the King Lay at Plimouth, mr de Soubise (having beene overthrowne by the king of frances navy, with the helpe of our English ships, lent them) came thither in distress, but the king would not look upon him. The rest of his forces were also dispersed.

The Same time also, the kings Ships that were sent out to scowre the coast of Turks and Dunkarks, which had don much hurt this Somer, brought in 10 prizes of Value into plimouth, of which one was very rich, having in her great quantity of silver, 8000 dozen of shooes, with other provision for Souldiers. Mr de Soubize was by king Charles his command confined unto mr Pawlets of Hinton, where now he is enterteined with great respect according unto his birth.

3 October
This day was chosen Bailiffes of dorchester.

William Whiteway, Senior 4.	Assistants.
Edmond Dashwood 3.	Joseph Paty.
Constables.	John Long.
Henry Derby, mercer.	Christopher way.
Joseph Underwood, Grocer.	Henry Derby.
Richard williams, Chandler.	Sherife.
Governour.	Mr Chaldecot, Esquire.
John Cooke, mercer.	Undersherife.
	Mr Goldsbery, tertio
	subvicecomite.

Memorandum that mr Edward Clark, who had beene Assistant unto mr white for 5 yeares, remooved to Tanton in July Last, and mr Nichols the younger came from Oxford now in October to supply his place.

4 October
This day the Navy set saile from Plimouth being 82 saile of English

ships, of which 11 were his Majestys and 20 Holland men of warre, with 12000 souldiers English, and 3000 old souldiers out of Holland. Sir Edward Cecill, Lord Generall, Set saile from Plimouth and the 9th day departed from falmouth towards their voiage.

7th dicto. The Duk of Buckingham and Earle of Holland having staid at Plimouth to See the fleet goe to sea, past through this towne, where no man knew them, nor took notice of them till they were gone.

The 11th of the same moneth they went towards the low Countrys, to receive of them the oath of allegiance, which they took on condicion that king Charles undertook to be their protector.

The 11th hereof, we had a presse for Levying of souldiers, 8 men in dorchester, but they went not away.

The 12 hereof died mr Henry Whittell one of our Aldermen, and Michael Humfrys, Esquire was chosen in his place 1st November.
About this tyme also died the Lord Sheffeld, Sir Thomas Smith, and Sir William Garraway of London.

26 October
The weekely fast on Wednesdays begun on the 20th July, ended in Dorchester this day with a contribution to the releife of Excester, which was in great distress, many dying for want and many weeke 100 and 150 of the sickenes. The collection that day was £23 16s to which was added £16 4s to mak up £40 and sent to Mr Ignatius Jordan who was left alone in Exon, of all the Magistrats, all the rest having forsaken them.

2 November
The lecture which had beene kept on Tuesday 20 yeare by mr White, in remembrance of the Gunpowder Treason, was this day settled upon Wednesday by occasion of the Wednesday fast.
Dr Williams, Bishop of Lincolne, Deane of Westminster and Lord keeper, was put from his Deanery, to which Succeeded Dr Bowle, first Deane of Sarum. And Sir Thomas Coventry was made Lord keeper. Sir Robert Heath was made Atturney generall. Mr Shelton was made Sollicitor.

1625

Michaelmas Terme was kept at Reading this yeare, where the king chose Shreives of Severall Counties, those that had beene most busy Last Parliament against giving any Subsidy at Oxford. Sir Edward Cooke for Buckinghamshire, Sir Guido Palmes for Rutland, Sir Thomas Wentworth for Yorks, Sir Robert Philips for Somersett, Sir francis Seimer for wiltes, that they might not trouble the next Parliament which tis said shalbe called shortly, on the refusing of the Privy seales by the countrey.

19th dicto died Robert Blandford servant to mr Gardner, having beene bitten by a mad dog 6 weeks before.

The king having commanded strict course to be taken with Papists, and ther houses to be searched for armour; the Lord Arundel of warder had 3 loade carried away from him. Lord Vaux resisted those that came to disarm him. And Sir Thomas Garret at the same time was Laid up in The Tower for som letteres intercepted between Spinola and him.

2 December

This day at 5 in the evening my second son John was borne, and baptised the 11th dicto. His sureties were my brother walker, Cousin Peter Middleton, and sister Elisabeth Bull. I pray God to make him his servant.

About the beginning of december our fleet began to returne homeward from Cales, where they had done nothing but taken Puntal, though the Earle of Essex and the rest of the Commanders were very ready and forward to any service. The souldiers when they came home, were billeted in Devonshire, as before their departure, and commanded not to depart from their colours. Sir Edward Cecill went for Ireland, where they say he is detayned prisoner by the Earle of Corke.

The end of this moneth, divers proclamations came forth, in which the king forbad all his subjects to trade with Spaine, or the Archduches countrey, and gave power to all men, to take any ship that they met carrying vitualls or munition unto them.

10 January 1625/6
This day the quarter sessions was held at Blandford, and in the
Commission of the peace, were left out many that had been Jus-
tices, to the number of [*blank*] whose names follow

> Doctor Goodwin
> Doctor wood [?excepd]
> Doctor whetcombe not put out
> George Browne, Esquire
> Mr Warre
> Leuston fitzjames, Esquire
> Mr Gallop, Esquire
> Henry Drake, Esquire
> Thomas Hussey, Esquire
> Mr Anketill, Esquire
> John Browne, Esquire
> Earle of Castlehaven

In this moneth the Privy seales came abroad of which 152 were for
Dorsett and in them 9 for Dorchester, Som £100.

17 January

	£		£
Sir francis Ashley	20	Humfrey Jolliffe	10
Mr John Gould	10	Widow Gould	10
Mr John Parkins	10	Leonard Meller	10
Mr William Whiteway	10	Mrs Chub	10
Mr Richard Blachford	10		
			100

30 January
The Summons for a Parliament to be holden at february 6th
Westminster. The knights of the Shire were chosen this day,
wherein though mr John Browne had more voices then Baronet
Morton, yet the Shrive mr Chaldicott slubberd up the busynes, and
returnd Baronet Morton, taking voices in a chamber.

Sir Thomas freke Sir George Morton, Baronet	} knights.
Michel Humfreys Richard Bushrod	} William Whiteway, Junior Dorchester
Sir John Strangeways Arthur Pine Giles Greene Barnard Michell	} Weymouth and Melcombe Regis.
Sir Lewys Dyves Sir Richard Strode	} Bridport
Sir Nathaniel Napper Edward Lawrence	} Wareham
Sir Robert Nappier Mr Edward Dacchum	} Corffe castle
Christopher Earle John Pine	} Poole
Sir Walter Earle Thomas Paramore	} Lyme
Samuel Turner William Whitaker	} Shaftesbury

This moneth died Sir Henry Hubbart, Lord cheife Justice of Common please, to whom succeeded Sir Thomas Richardson.

This same moneth came 100 old soldiers out of the Low Countrys, which the Duke of Buckingham obteined out of the States, to muster and traine all the companies in England. Of these 100 two are sent unto Every Shire to be resident.

2 February
This day king Charles was crowned at Westminster, with great solemnity. The Queen refused to be Crowned by any Protestant Bishop, without dispensation from the Pope. There were now Created 8 Earles and 80 knights of the Bath. The solemnity of the kings riding through London in State is put of to the 1st May next coming.

6 February
This day the Parliament began at Westminster in which the king exhorted them, to insist mainely upon the establishing of relligion, and providing that all men might be taught, as also to have regard unto the kingdome, that it may bee fortified. But when they began

to sit, they met with many foule elections which tooke up much time. Amongst the rest Baronet morton was put out of the house, and a new writ sent downe to choose another knight for Dorsett upon the 27th february, where was chosen Sir George Morton againe.

Sir Edward Coke also and Sir francis Seymor, whome the king had made Shreives, were chosen to be of the house, but the king desired the house to put them out. Who would not put them out of their nomber, but were content to spare their presence, in regard of their offices of shreives.

They fell out with the high Commission court, about Sir Thomas Howard, who being of the lower house was detained prisoner by them for Incontinency with the Vicountess of Purbec.

But amongst all others, one cheife busyness that they took in hand, was to looke into the managing of the Late fleete that went out, and of the causes of the bad successe, which they could not enter into without fastening upon the Duke. Another thing also that drew him into question was the generall seasure of all English goods in france, which happened at this time, by meanes of a french ship of Newhaven, value £40000, detained by the Duke.

28 February
This day ½ an houre after 6 in the morning god tooke unto himselfe, my second son John, about 3 moneths old, when he had not beene sicke above 3 houres.

6 March
This day the Assises were holden for this County by Sir John walter, Lord cheife Baron, and Baron Denham, the first being in Parliament, went not the circuit though he were in the Commission. The Assises for Devon was held at Tiverton.

The same day died in Dorchester at Henry Brownes house, Mr Henry Collier suddenly. He had beene marshall to Judge fenner, and since, by usury, gott an estate of more than £20000 but was lately growne Lunatick, and beyd for a foole.

About the beginning of this moneth, there was a very great inundation in Andalusia in Spayne, by which Sevill was drowned, with a great circuit round about, and in it 40 or 50000 head of Cattell, many 1000 of houses overborne by the water.

[80]

5 March
This day the Earle of Arundel was sent Prisoner to the Tower, for marrying his eldest son to the sister of the young duke of Lenox, without his Majesties Leave, as it is pretended, released soone after, and confined to his house in the Country.

3 April 1626
This day mr Michel Humfreies died in London. Being one of the Capitall Burgesses of Dorchester, and at present one of our Burgesses for the Parliament. In his steed was chosen for Capitall Burgesses of Dorchester Mr William Derby, upon the 10th Aprill, and Burgess for the Parliament, william whiteway, junior, upon the 19th dicto.

[May]
The fift of this moneth the Parliament, having begun to question the Duke, and beene forbidden by the king, but still resuming courage, was prorogued unto the 13th of the same. Where they met againe, and fell into consideration of divers misdemeanors committed by him, which they reduced into these articles.
1. His plurality of offices.
2. Oppressing the East India Company.
3. Buying and selling of offices.
4. Not guarding the narrow seas.
5. The wrongfull Stay of the Peter of Newhaven.
6. Delivering over of our ships to the french.
7. Sending them against Rochell.
8. Compelling the Lord Roberts to buy honour.
9. Procuring honours for his poore kindred, who must be mainteyned by the king.
10. Intercepting and exhausting the kings revenues.
11. His applying Physicke to king James a little before his death. These articles were charged against him to the Lords in the Painted chamber by 8 of the lower house who amplified them.
   Sir dudley digs the preamble.
   Mr Herbert   Mr Selden
   Mr Glanvile   Mr Pim
   Mr Sherland   Mr Wainsford
   Sir John Elliot the conclusion.

[81]

This was so closely applied, that the first and the Last within 2 daies after were sent to the Tower by the king upon some misinformations, but when the house stood upon their priviledges and would not proceede in any busynesse, till their members were released, they were soone restored to them.

Besides this the Earle of Bristoll accused the said Duke of high Treason in the upper house, upon 12 articles, of which his son presented a copy to this lower house. To all these the Duke had time and counsell appointed him to frame an answere, which he delivered in, the beginning of June, very sleightly framed. Thereunto the lower house were making a reply. But the king changed the reading of the bill of 4 Subsidys which the house had promised to give, that upon their refusall, the Parliament was dissolved upon the 15th day of June. The house refused to pass the act for Subsidies, onely for a time till the Greivances might be presented to the king and answered. But the king would not admit of any delaies, nor of any conditions.

17 June
This day the Earle of Bristoll was sent to the Tower, prisoner for no other knowne cause, but because he had in the Parliament, accused the Duke of high Treason.

Towards the end of this session the house had penned a declaration to shew to the king the carridge of busynesses by the duke, and the ground why they could not presently pass the subsidies. But the king would not heare it, but presently upon the dissolution commanded by proclamation, that no man should read it, nor keepe it, nor give any copy of it.

The king being thus destitute of mony to furnish his necessities sent to the Londoners to borrow of them £100000. They refused him twice plainely, that they had no mony, by meanes of the deadness of trade. At last the Aldermen lent £24000.

During this Parliament the Earle of Suffolk died, who was Chancellour of Cambridge. In whose place the University chose the duke, to the great offence and dislike of the Parliament who, if they had sate, had questioned them about it. Ther died also the Bishops of Exeter, of Carlile, and of Bath and Wells.

This somer there died Mrs Alice Pitt of Weymouth, Mr John Early and Mrs Joane Adin of Dorchester.

The Lord Lieutenant of Dorset being dead, his son the young

Earle of Suffolk succeeded him. Who named his Deputys, Sir Thomas freake, Sir John Browne, Sir Nathaniel Napper, and Mr Hastings.

July
The report was very hot of the coming of the Spaniards. Whereupon the king, having no mony to set forth a navy, sent abroad warrants to the port townes to set out men of warre, and amongst others, for 3 men of warre out of this County. And to the londoners hee commanded to furnish 12000 souldiers with armour, horses, and all munition at ther owne charges. He also sent unto the merchants strangers of London for a lone of £50000. And being refused in all these, commanded the Londoners upon ther allegiance to furnish out 20 men of warre, to guard the coast, which they did.

25 July
Luk Edwards of Melcome died, having Lately come from Caen, which made him suspected to dy of the sickeness, but it prooved otherwise.

27 July
This day the Assises were held in Dorchester by Sir John Walter, Lord cheife Baron, and Baron Denham. At this time, Sir John Strangewaies, and Sir walter Earle, with many others, are put out of the Commission of the peace for being so busy last Parliament.

2 August
This day was held a generall fast, proclaimed before by the king, upon which the weather, which had beene all the Somer unseasonable, was turned into a very faire harvest.

Quartercrownes having past currant ever since the king [?Received] his marriage mony in them, were now descried.

The 8th hereof, the Justices sate about a Benevolence to the king to supply his wants, in which was very little given and that which was given, was by Papists and Popish persons.

The Duk of Buckinghams daughter is contracted to the Earle of Montgomerys sonne.

At this time all the french that attended about the queene, were

[83]

sent away. Save her nurse and her daughter, and her English Prieste.

15 August
The sickenes began to breake out in Blandford, very dangerously, and within 10 daies after at Bridport, and spread into many parishes thereabouts. At Blandford there died in all some 20 persons. In Bridport 70. It was suspected also againe to be in Weymouth.

At this time there was new coine made both of gold and silver, lighter by £7 10s per [?ounce] then the former, but was called in againe within three weekes.

25th dicto a company of marryners set upon the Duke of Buckingham in the streets of London, and demanded pay, which he was glad to give them to rid himselfe out of their hands.
    After the Benevolence, followed privy seales, but both being refused, the king by proclamation remittd all those that had refused to pay, and also all that had promised.

3 September
About this time the souldiers of the last yeares fleete which had layen ever since about Plimouth, were now remooved and billeted all along the sea coast, as far as Sussex and Kent. A thousand of them, of the regiment of the Earle of Essex were billeted in the County of dorsett.
    The Earle of Holland is made Master of the Horse. The Earle of Barkshire, Warden of the Cinq ports. Robert Bateman, Chamberlain of London.

About this time the king of denmark [?Received] a great overthrow by Tilly, and saved himself by flight in the Dukdome of Brunswicke, and having shortly after recovered good strength was againe overthrowne by the said Tilly in another Battell, and wholly put to rout, and had much adoo to escape into his owne Country.

25th September died. Dr Andrews Bishop of winchester. Mr Desdiguieres Constable of france. John Swichard Archbishop of Mentz, one of the princes electors in Germany.

1626

2 October
Bailiffs for dorchester chosen.

Bailiffs	Assistants
Richard Bushrod 3.	Joseph Underwood.
John Blachford 1.	Amias Martin.
Constables.	Henry Maber.
Richard Williams, Chandler.	George Mondin.
Richard Bury, Grocer.	Sheriffe of dorsett.
George wey, Glover.	Sir William Uvedall, knight.
Governour.	Undersheriff.
Henry Derby, mercer.	John Cole, the second time.

Gondemar, having been emploied in an Embassage to france, died in his returne towards Spaine.

27 October
Sir Thomas Yorke, lieutenant Colonel to the Earle of Essex, came downe into this country, to take charge of his Regiment, which is billeted about this Towne. Dorchester gave him 40s per weeke towards his enterteynment and 16s per weeke to other officers.

30 October
The young Marquis Hamilton, being discontent with the Duke of Buckingham, rode post into Scotland, and standeth upon his guard.

November
In this moneth, the Subsidy Roiall went about, which all the Judges refused to subscribe unto, and som of them were thereupon put from their places, as Sir Randall Crew, from being Lord cheife Justice of the kings Bench. The Lawyers of the Innes of court refused also, and many Lords, led by thexample of the Earle of Warwicke. These refused to subscribe, but the greatest part of them paid ther money. In steed of Sir Randall Crew, Sir Nicholas Hide was made Lord cheife Justice kings bench.

Sir Thomas Richardson, kings Sergeant, paid £16000 for the office of Lord cheif Justice of the Common plais, which had beene long void, and had it.

The 27th of this moneth, my Aunt Middelton of Periplace died.

This same time, my father bought a lease of Ashdon farme, of 3 lives, of my Lord of Suffolke. The lives that are upon the Lease are,

My brothers John and Samuel Whiteway, and my sonne William Whiteway. And my father Parkins bought three lives in the farme of Clandon at the same time.

4 December
This day Thomas Devenish, Serjeant, was made keeper of the Common Jaile, and Benjamin Derby chosen Sergeant in his place the 15th december.

10 December
The sickenes was suspected to be in the house of Paul a hatter of this towne, because 3 of his house died in 15 daies, and his house was shut up 5 or 6 weekes, but god be praised, it was not so, but as it is supposed, some pestilentiall feaver.

1627

1 January 1626/7
Mr Whites morning lecture was encreased from Mondaies and fridaies, to Mondaies, Tuesdaies, and fridaies.

3 January
I, W.W. was chosen Steward of the Hospitall, in the place of mr Toope, and George Gould was chosen Governour, in the place of George Wey.

This winter, the Church of All Saints in dorchester, was enlarged. Count Mansfeld died at Spalata in dalmatia, travelling to Venice.

The 13th January the Earle of Suffolke and Sir Robert Nanton, master of the Court of wards, came downe into Dorsett, for the setting forward of the Lone, which amounted to 5 subsidies, and all men in this County subscribed thereunto, except Sir John Strangewaies, Sir walter Earle, Mr Tregonwell, Mr william Savidge, Atturney.

These 4 were, for refusing, bound to answere it at the Counsell table, from whence the three former were sent prisoners to the fleete, and the last unto the new prison in Clarkenwell. Divers others of other counties also were committed to severall prisons for the same busynes, and among others the Earle of Lincolne. But in some counties, the commons refused generally to lend, and were all dismissed, the Counsell not knowing what course to take with them.

The 17th January, here was held an extraordinary Commission for the tryall of som souldiers in which Sir francis Ashley sate Judge, and condemned 7 souldiers and one tapster to death, for burglary, but 6 of the souldiers had a pardon.

In this moneth, many Spanish men of war, bound with men and money for flanders, were cast away upon the coast of Brittaine in france, and three rich Caracks at the Groine in Galicia.

[87]

3 February

This day the marriners of the kings ships assembled in great troupes, and marched furiously through London to Whitehall, and demanded there pay, with many threats against the Duke, insomuch that he was faine to muster the traine souldiers of middlesex, and put them in armes, and yet give the marriners good words, and ther pay also, to be rid of them.

The 10th hereof 4 German Gentlemen, all of the Palatinate, being banished for Relligion, came hither for shelter, and were here enterteined. Their names are, Mr Sleer, Mr Fisher, Mr Hanke, and Mr Hopff.

The 13th hereof, the barne at Eglisham was burnt, by means of a dier called Crandon that lived in it.

The 26th hereof, the Assises were held in Dorchester, by Baron Denham. Sir John Walter, Lord cheife Baron was in the same Commission, but could not come, for the Gout. Mr Hemor preached.

12 March

This day my Unkle John Pit of Bridport died, being 80 yeares old. He died of age, and of the Stone. This day my Cousin James Gould and I did ride to London, to Joine with the merchants of Exeter, in petitioning the king and the Counsell, that we might have as much french goods delivered us as we had arrested in france.

The 16th hereof, the Duke of Buckingham his onely son died, and being cut up, was found to have his liver exceedingly swollen.

[March] 1627

The 29th hereof, the Archdeacon visited, and mr Ball of Purbec preched.

1 Aprill

The outports were commanded to furnish ships of war to defend the coasts at ther owne charges. Weymouth, Poole, and Lime were to set out 2 but they refused.

This Spring was very dry, little raine fell from february to June, but all the Somer afterwards was very full of Raine.

[88]

18th. There was great Preparation made for a fleete, 60 ships prepared, the Duke promised to goe in person, many Land souldiers
were prest for that service, 250 in Dorset, and 15 daies after 100
more, and a moneth after 150 more.

The king sent unto the Londoners about the Lone, but they
refused to pay it. The sickenesse began in Salisbury and grew very
hot, continued there until December next winter – in which there
died 500 persons at least.

10 May
This day the souldiers of the Earle of Essex, and my Lord of Valen-
tias Regiment, billeted in this country, remooved towards Southampton, and had each of them 8s from his Landlord, which was a
great ease to the people. The Captaines were paid a moneth before
at Southampton by the King.

21th hereof a woman was slaine, by mischance, by a sledge that one
was casting which beate out her braines.

In this moneth, all trade between England and france was quite
shut up upon former quarrells. The french forbad the bringing in
of all English Commoditys on paine of Confiscation, and the king
of England forbad, that no goods should be brought out of france
in a french bottome upon like penalty. Many frenchmen were
brought in by letter of mart, and made prizes.

21 May
I tooke Mr Thomas Brownes house for 7 yeares at £10 per annum.

24 May
Mr John Coke was made Lieutenant, Henry Derby Ensigne,
Henry Browne Sergeant Major, and Amias Martin yonger
sergeant of Captain Pelhams company.

5 June
There was a third press generall in this County, 150 to serve the
king in this fleete.

11 June
Sir John Strangewaies, prisoner in the fleete, had liberty for 5
weekes to come into the Countrey, granted him.

[89]

This moneth the order of the Garter was sent to the King of Sweden, and to Henry Frederic Prince of Orange, but the latter made some difficulty to accept it, for feare least the french, with whome wee are at ods, should take them to favour the English, onely: yet they accepted it at last.

23 June
This day Captain Champion of Weymouth brought in a prize, a Brasill man with 100 chests of Sugar, and a weeke after Captain Lockier with a Bristow man brought home two Spanish prises, of which one was worth £20000. Captaine Lockier was to have ⅓ the Bristow man ⅔.

27 June
This day the fleete set saile from Portsmouth being 96 saile, the Duk Generall, Monsieur de Soubise with him. They had 7000 Land souldiers. The king came to Portesmouth to see them goe to the sea.

The 12th July they came to the Isle of Ré, where at their landing they were furiously encountred by 200 french horse, and many of them driven into the sea and drowned, and among others 20 Captaines and Lieutenants. But at last the french were repulsed with the loss of 125 horse, and 250 foote.

About 15 dayes after, the fort of St Martins was yeelded up unto them, the french departing with white rods in their hands whereupon there followed a generall press here in England to supply the Dukes army. 2 were prest in Dorchester. Ther were 500 men sent also to defend Garnesey and Garsey, which the french do threaten to invade.

July
The king of Denmark arrested all the English goods at Hamburg, for £70000 he lent to king James, but the arrest continued not long, and the goods were released.

12 July
By meanes of the sickenes at Salisbury, the Assises were held this day at Sherborne for Dorset, by Sir John Walter Lord cheife Baron, and Sir John Denham, at Andover for Hamshire, and at Warminster for wilts.

The archbishop Canterbury was confined to his house, for refusing to approove Dr Sibthorpes sermon of Catholike obedience and Dr Lawde, Bishop [of] Bath and wells had the administracion of his archbishoprik.

15 July
Mr John Pawlet was created Baron of Hinton in Somersetshire.

2 August
Cousin Peter Middelton went from hence, to be a Turkey merchant, having lived here three yeares.

9 August
The King sent for all the Counsell to Winsor, to consult about a Parliament, but at that time it tooke no effect.

26 August
Mr ferdinand Nicols went hence to live at Sherborne and within a moneth after, Mr Whitefield succeeded him in his assistance to Mr White.

September
In this moneth there died Cousin Rawlin Haine 4th dicto. Mrs Morice of Melcombe 6 dicto. Sister Martha Parkins 16 dicto.

8 September
Woodbery faire was forbidden this yeare in regard of the plague at Sarum. Last yeare for Blandford, and the yeare before for London.

18 September
There were 5000 men provided to be sent to the Isle of St Martins for supplyes to the Duke of Buckingham.
   This day the Lord Willmot past through this towne, towards Plimmouth about that service.

29 September
This day Martha Adin was married to Edward Brag and 3 daies after Thomas Blachford to Margaret Meech.

[91]

1 October
Bailives were chosen for
Dorchester.
    Mr Richard Blachford,
    m[erchant].   Governour.
    Mr James Gould 1.   John Long, Bookeseller.
Constables.   Assistants.
    George way, Glover.   Robert Coker.
    Matthew Butler,   Simon Hasilbury.
    Shooemaker.   Richard Savidge.
    Henry Maber, Clothier.   Henry Derby.

4 October
I began to keepe house this day.[10]
    This moneth there died neare us. Mr Giles Meller the 5th. Mr
Robert Cheeke the 8th. Sir John Browne the 10th. Old Lady Tren-
chard the 16th.
    Leuston fitzjames Esquire was this year Sherife of Dorsett. His
Undersheriffe was Mr Golseney the younger.

19 October
This day here was another press of men to goe to St Martins with
the Earle of Holland, to helpe the Duke, whose army was growne so
weake, that before the Earle of Holland came to him, he was set
upon in his trenches and lost 2000 men, amongst them many Captains, 4 Colonels, and others of great command. Lord Monjoy, and
Lord Gray and some others were taken prisoners. So the 16th of
November the Duke came home with a few men, and those in very
bad plight, and left 30000 ton of wine, and a very great quantity of
Salt in the Iland. Yet was he well entertained at the Court, as if he
had done excellent service.

22 November
This day Sir Walter Earle, Mr Corriton, and some other Gentelmen that had long beene prisoners in the fleet about the Lone, almost a whole yeare, got a Habeas corpus out of the kings bench, to
be tried there, and so they were, Mr Ley being their cheife Lawyer,
who defended them so well, that he convinced all the assistants that
they had wrong. Yet the Kings atturney craved time to certify the
king of it and so their delivery was protracted.

1627

The 22th hereof died Mr John Wats, and the 30th hereof died his daugher Mrs Bushrode and Mrs Lee 7th december.

27 November

This day was an extraordinary great tempest of wind, which blew downe many houses and great trees, cast away 2 of the kings ships, and 7 others of the fleet at Plimmouth. And in Deed, all this quarter was full of great stormes, and much raine, in one of which 50 sail of Colliers were cast away upon the north coasts. And all this quarter of the yeare was full of great stormes of wind, and much raine.

December

In the beginning of this moneth Dr Preston was banished the Court for preaching plainly against Idolatry, and many ministers of London suspended, and some imprisoned for preaching against the evills of the time.

At this time, Mr Hugh Pine was imprisoned in the Gatehouse at Westminster, for saying his shephard would make as good a King as King Charls, but it was not prooved and so he was soone released.

Our Prisoners were freely released in france and Came home, Lord Montjoy etc.

7 December

The King borrowed of the Londoners £120000 for which and £244000 due to them before, he engaged a great deale of Land.

16 December

Mr Samuel Whitefield was chosen Parson of All Saints in Mr Cheeks place, and Mr Rulizius succeeded him in assistance to Mr White. He was inducted the 11 January.

4 January 1627/8
The souldiers that came from St Martins, and Lay in Devonshire, were remooved Eastward, two Regiments, in both 500 men, namely Sir Thomas Frier, and Sir Henry Spryes into Dorset, and of them 36 into this towne. But Sir Henry Spries Regiment were within one moneth remooved hence into Glocestershire.

11 January
Sir John Strangeways, Sir Walter Earle, and all the rest that were imprisoned for the Lone, were this day set at liberty after allmost a yeares imprisonment.

The 13th hereof Sir Anthony Ashly died.

The 18th Mrs Chub died, and gave all her lands and goods to Mr Coker the Goldsmith, and to a little boy of his called Matthew Chub, upon condition that he should mary with Joane, second daughter to mr Coker.

14 January
Seing Mr Langley could not come to live here, mr Brancard of Shaston was desired to teach the scholers, till some other were chosen Schoolemaster.

29 January
This day Cousin Thomas Newman was maried.

4 February
This day a Parliament was summoned to begin at Westminster the 17th Martii, and the privy seales were called in, that had lately beene sent abroad.

20 February
This day my son John the second, was borne ¼ after 1 in the afternoone, and baptised the 24th, Mr James Gould, and my brother Parkins, and my Mother Whiteway being his sureties. And the 22th

of the same, god took to his mercy my daughter Margaret being about 3 yeares and halfe old.

About this time the mariners againe grew very insolent and disorderly about the Court, for want of pay, they assaulted the Duk in his house, braved the Judges in Westminster hall, and rifled the Lord Treasurers house, so that the Duke durst not goe abroad without a guard. Mr Noy quieted them.

At this time two Ambassadors came from the States into England, and two others into France, as it is thought, to reconsile the two kingdoms.

25 February
This day the Knights of the Shire were chosen for the Parliament, as followeth. Sir John Strangewaies. Sir Walter Earle.

for dorchester.
  Densell Holles, Esquire.
  John Hill, marchant.
for Weymouth and Melcombe.
  Sir Lewys Dive.
  Sir Robert Nappier.
  Hugh Pine, Recorder.
  Henry Waltham, marchant.
for Shaftesbury.
  Sir John Croke.
  William Whitaker, esquire.
for Lyme.
  Thomas Paramour.
  Christopher Earle, Esquire.

for Wareham.
  Sir John Meller.
  Gerrard Napper, Esquire.
for Corffe.
  Sir francis Nethersoll.
  Giles Greene.
for Bridport.
  John Browne Esquire.
  Francis Drake, Esquire.
  Bamfield Chaffin.
  Captain Paulet.
for Poole.
  Sir John Cooper, Baronet.
  John Pine Esquire.

The choise of Bridport was questioned in the Parliament and overthrowne, and two new chosen, ut supra.

10 March
This day the Assises were holden here by Justice Denham alone. The Lord cheife Baron being stayed for the Parliament. Mr Wilkinson preached.

17 March
This day the Parliament beganne at Westminster, in which the King shewd that he had drawne them together to supply his necessary occasions for the warres. Sir John Finch was chosen speaker.

The Archbishop of Canterbury, the Bishop of Lincolne, the Earles of Arundel, Lincolne and Bristoll were restored to the upper house: some Lords put out for refusing the oath of Supremacy. The Commons began to vindicate their liberty, and withall promised the King 5 Subsidys, which he tooke very kindly. They obtained of the King a proclamation for a publike fast, for their better successe, which was kept in London the 5th Aprill and in the rest of the Kingdome upon the 21th of the same. Then they fell to complaining of the lone, and billetting of souldiers, and drew a petition, which they called a petition of rights, for the expressing of our liberties, and the confirmation of Magna charta. Which after many delayes and much adoe, was at last solemnely granted by the King in the upper house, both houses being present, in these words: Soit droit faict come est desiré. [*May justice be done as asked.*] This was the 7th June.

April 1628
The 11th of this moneth, the souldiers billetted in Dorset, remooved hence towards Plimouth, to goe thence for Rochell with the Earle of Denbigh, but they were left behind, and so returned to be billetted in this County againe. And so they were all, except the 23 that had beene billetted in Dorchester, which were now refused, though Sir Thomas Frier their Colonel obteyned Letters from the Counsell to the Towne, and procured a Commission to Sir Thomas Trenchard, Sir John Brewen, John Browne, and Henry Drak, Esquire for the examining of Mr Bushrod as an agent in [detering] other men from billetting. But it came to nothing.

14 April
This day I was chosen overseer of the Poore for Trinity parish together with mr Joseph Underwood.

The 22th hereof Sir francis Ashley was imprisoned by the Lords house for speaking against the liberty of the subject, but upon his recantacion, and craving of pardon, he was soone released. Mannering also a great Arminian Divine, was in the begining of June Imprisoned, fined, degraded, and his books burnt, for some seditious speeches against the liberty of the Subjects.

The 25th hereof the Earle of Denbigh went to sea to Releive

Rochell which was still hardly beseeged by sea and Land. He had neare 30 men of warre, and 30 vitailers, but when he came in sight of the Towne, he said he had no commission to hazard the Kings ships in fight, and so returned shamefully to Portesmouth the 16th of May. Where the King gave order to have the fleete newly fitted up and sent thither againe.

The 3rd of May the sickeness brake out in Shaftesbury and in some other places thereabouts, but spred not far, nor continued very long, there died not above some 20 persons in all.

This Spring died.
> Dr Matthewes Archbishop of yorke.
> The Earle of Worcester Lord Privy seale.
> Dr Carleton Bishop of Chichester.   .
> Cousin Joane Kebbell 29th May.
> Mary Toope 31th dicto.
> Mr Ironside the elder, preacher.
> Mr Frencham preacher 18th June.
> The Earle of Devonshire in June.
> Mr Richard Bushrod 1st July.
> Mr Samuel Whitfield 5th July.

[?1] June
This day mr Rives the Schoolemaister came to this towne, the place having beene supplied by Mr Brancard, ever since Mr Cheekes death till now. Mr Brancards brother was chosen his Usher, and Mr Tutchin was Vicar of fordington. Mr Pele Parson of Compton.

13 June
Dr Lambe the witch was beaten to death in London streetes by the boyes and apprentises.

20 June
This day the lower house presented their Remonstrance to the King, which he took in ill part, and thereupon they went about to make a second declaracion against the Duke, but the king prevented them and dissolved the parliament, the 26th June, till the 20th of October next. The 5 Subsidys were granted, all of them paiable within 8 moneths.

14 July

This day Mr Richard Hening and his family came to this towne to dwell.

In this moneth the Earle of Manchester was made Lord privy seale. The Earle of Marleburgh, Lord President, and Sir Richard Weston, Lord Treasurer, and the Earle of Suffolke, Lord Warden of the Cinq ports.

About the end of this moneth the Earle and Countess of Suffolk came to Lullworth Castle, and staid there 2 monthes, where she was brought to bed of a daughter. The 11 of August he sent a bucke to this Towne.

31 July

This day was the Assises at Dorchester before Sir John Walter, and Sir John Denham. Mr Gillingham preached.

August

The beginning of this moneth, the King came to Portesmouth to hasten the setting forth of the fleet for Rochell, in which the Duke should have gon Generall, but after some insolencys of the mariners committed against him, for which 1 was hangd by Martiall Law, and 2 others killd by the Duke and his followers, the 23th of this moneth the Duk himself was killd with a knife by John Felton, who Justified his act, saying he had done god and his Countrey good service. Upon the Dukes death the Earle of Lindsey was chosen Admiral of the fleete. The Earle of Holland Chancellor of Cambridge and Baily of Westminster.

3 September

This day Mr Bailifs appointed the Beadle to cut and carry away the Corne that fordington men had sowne upon the Towne Walles.

The 1st of this moneth the Lord Brook was stabd by his man, and died therof about a moneth after. His man having stabd him, killd himselfe also.

8 September

This day the fleete set saile from Portesmouth, commanded by the Earle of Linsey, and consisting of 100 saile besides fireships and vitailers. They went to releive Rochell, which was beseeged by the french both by sea and Land, and attempted often to releive it, but could not get in for the palissade that was made by the French athwart the harbour. But the 20th October the Citty was yeelded to the King, and but 4000 Persons alive in it, 18000 being dead with famine. Thereupon our fleete returned and by stormes and foule weather lost [*entry unfinished*]

22 September
This day Mr Richard Savidge was chosen to be of the company in steed of Mr Richard Bushrod deceased.

24 September
This day all the traine bands of this division and Bridport and Sherborne divisions mustered together at Madbury downs.

6 October
This day were chosen Bailiffs.
   Bernard Toup 2.
   William Whiteway, Junior 1.
Constables.
   Henry Maber, Clothier.
   John Allimbrig, Clothier.
   Josias Terry, Haberdasher.
Shreife of Dorsett.
   Thomas Still, Esquire.

Governour.
   Richard Bury, Grocer.
Assistants.
   Joseph Underwood.
   George Mundyn.
   Richard Williams.
   Henry Derby.
Undersheriffe.
   Rinaldo Knapton.

John Williams of Heringston, Esquire was chosen to be Captaine of the Horse for this Division, insteed of Sir John Meller.

6 October
This day William Paty was married unto Margaret the daughter of Mr Robert Coker of this Towne.

20 October
This day the Parliament was againe adjourned to the 20th January next.

November
The fleete being returned home from Rochell, the souldiers were all disbanded and sent home to their owne dwellings.

The end of this yeare there died.
>Dr Mountaine Archbishop of Yorke.
>Mr Hugh Pine, Counsellor.
>The wife of Mr John Humfrys, 1st November.
>William Chaffy 26th November.
>Mr Ducke, Recorder of Exon.
>Mr Edward Gould of Coome in Devon.
>Bernard Toope 12th december.
>The wife of Mr William Jolliffe 27th dicto.
>Mr Phineas Pit 31th dicto.

22 November
This day Mr John Ball of Langton was instituted and inducted to the parsonage of All Saints in Dorchester in the place of mr Whitfield.

28 November
This day John Felton was condemned at Westminster, and hanged at Tiborne for killing the Duke of Buckingham.

Thomas Devenish was put out of the Keepers place, and Thomas Sparrow made Keeper in his steed. Yet Thomas Devenish kept the house of correction still, and had £40 per annum allowed him of the County for it.

At this time Sir John Strangeways and Sir Walter Earle were againe made Justices of the peace, having beene put by for more then 2 yeares.

December
This yeare Sir George Trenchard kept a very great Christmas at Wolton, and on Twelfe day, maried his youngest daughter to Mr Champernon.

The 12th of this moneth Mr White began to expound the Bible the second time.

In this moneth the inhabitants of the forest of Gillingham rose up against those which went about to inclose it and afterwards overthrew their works, and misused the Bailyes that were sent thither with suppenas to serve them. But this stir was soone quieted by the Shreives.

21 December
This day mr Endymion Porter, a gentleman of the Kings bed-
chamber, coming out of Spaine in a Spanish Ship, was cast away at
Burton neare Bridport, but all the men were saved, being 100
Spaniards, and were all of them billeted by Sir Thomas freke at
Horseyes Melcombe for 5 weekes and then sent to Portsmouth to
be shipt home. The goods of the ship were pillaged, but were most
of them restored upon the Counsells letters.

7 January 1628/9

This day the king of Bohemia his eldest son Fredericus Henricus, 15 yeares old, was drowned neare Amsterdam, being going thither to behold the triumphs of the reception of the West India fleete brought in by Peter Haine. The English Court mourned for him.

This moneth, there came order from the Counsell to levy 15 men out of every traine band, to be ready to goe for Garnesey when need required.

There died about this time. William Lord Marquis Winchester. Gilbert Raleigh Viceadmiral Dorset. Thomas Walker of Exon, Esquire. Sir francis Ashley was taken sicke of a palsey at London but recovered.

Robert Napper Esquire was made Viceadmirall of Dorset in steed of Mr Raleigh.

20 January

This day the Parlement met again at Westminster: where the Kings first proposition was for the settling of the Bill of Tonnage and Poundage. But the house resolved to settle Relligion, and to provide for the suppressing of Popery and Arminianisms, before they would conclude of any other busynesse. They discovered also a formall Colledge of Jesuites at London, but could not have the Law executed against them, for all of them had procured pardons. Then the Parlement obtained of the King a generall fast. Kept at London 18th february, and over all England the 20th March. And so went on till the 23 february when the Lower house adjourned themselves for two daies. The King being offended at that, adjourned them for 7 daies, and then when they met, for 10 daies more, where there was much adoe about the adjournment in the lower house. Mr Hollis and Mr Valentine kept the speaker in his chaire by force: and Sir John Elliot voted the 3 articles of Liberty in the house. Thereupon on the 10th March the King in great anger dissolved the Parlement, and sent 5 of the lower house to the Tower, one to the fleete, and another to the gatehouse, and 14 daies after published a Declaration of the causes that moved him to dissolve the Parlement etc.

5 february
This day mr King was chosen Recorder of Weymouth, by the practise of David Giar, Maior, whereas the place was promised to mr Christopher Earle.

16 February
This day mr Joseph Pit was maried.

5 March
This day the assises were held here by Baron Denham alone, the Lord cheife Baron attending the Parlement.

At this time Captaine Pelham resigned his place, and Captain William Napper succeeded him in it.

About this time newes came abroad that the Queene was with child, and 15th March bonfires were made in London for it, and a prayer printed for her safe delivery. She was afterwards delivered of a man child at Greenewich the 13 day of May, but the child was borne dead, and buried the next day at Westminster.

20 March
This day was a generall fast kept over all the Kingdome, by the Kings proclamation, and in London the 18th february before.

28 March 1629
This day Mr Richard Henning left the towne, and Mr Browne came hither the 18 Aprill after.

16 Aprill
This day Mr William Coker Esquire came to live in this Towne.

The 5th of this moneth Thomas Sparrow Jailekeeper died, and his son in Law Knapton kept the Jaile.

In this moneth Mr John Browne set up Mr Hardys monument in St Peters Church, but the towne paid for it £5.

5 May
This day Mr Robert Angel maried my Cousin Susan Bateman.

10 May
This day peace was proclaimed betweene England and France, both at London and at Paris, after 2 or 3 yeares warres.

11 May
This day there was a white Circle seen about the Sun, after which followed much faire and dry and hot weather for a long season.

19 May
This day Jeffery Neve came hither with the Kings commission about the setting up of Archery.

Upon the declaration made by the lower house of Parlement at their breaking up, that those that paid Custome before it were granted by Parliament, were enemyes to the state, there was a generall refusall in London and other places to pay any Custome. The King and the Lord Treasurer used many motives to perswade the merchants to trade, and at length prevailed with some, who thereupon wer much hated and hardly spoken of by the rest of their neighbours.

2 June
Mr Clement Walker of Cliffe stabd his wife with his knife, as they sate at dinner.

14 June
John Thorlton died suddeinly.

18 June
Sir Thomas Edmonds went this day extraordinary Embassador for france, about the ratification of the peace, and eight daies after Monsieur des Preaux the french Ambassador came to London to the same purpose. Where they were put off from their audience on both sides, because the French would have the English make a league offensive and defensive, and so blocke up the way to the peace with Spaine, which was treated of by the English, notwithstanding the Earnest solicitation of the French, Hollanders and Venetians to the contrary.

This somer the Prince of Orange bessegd Shertrogenbosch with a great army and in September took it.

The french King having taken some townes in Languedoc,

made peace with the Protestants of that Countrey, and bent his forces against the Spaniards and Imperialls about Mantova.

10 July
This day was the battell fought in fleetstreete betweene the Templers and the Cittizens in which 6 were slain and 80 wounded. The King appointed a speciall commission to sit upon it in which the Lord cheife Justice and others were Commissioners: Captain Stanford, and Captaine Ashenhurst, being the ringleaders, were hanged at Tiburne 24 July.

21 July
This day mr Bushrod was maried to my sister Willmot Parkins, and the 28 dicto Mr Robert Blake to Mary Dashwood; both of them proved Bankrupts Within a yeare and halfe.

27 July
This day the Regiments of Dorchester, Sherborne, and Bridport were mustered alltogether at Madbury downe, when Captain Napper went first into the field.

23 July
This day the Assises were held here by Lord Chief Baron Walter, and Baron Denham. Mr Mayo preached.

3 August
This day there was a foule outrage comitted by the Gentlemen of Lincolns Inn upon a pursivant thither to apprehend one that had killed one of the Kings Deere. They shaved him, snipt his eare, washt him in the kennell, and kicked him out at the gate. The King tooke it much to hart.

9 August
This day my unkle John Mounsell came into England, and staid here 6 moneths.

11 August
This day Mr William Benne was inducted Parson of All Saints, the place being vacant by the resignation of Mr John Ball, who returned to Langton.

12 August
This day Mr Thomas Still Sherife of Dorset, sent for 30 of this
towne to disarme the Rebells about Gillingham, when there was no
occasion.

21 August
This day the wind was so high, that it tore a coach all in pieces upon
Eggardon hill, and beate out the braines of a waiting maid that was
in it.

This moneth the Hollanders having surprised Wesell, and being
much distressed by the invasion of their enemyes, and busyed in
the siege of Shertogenbosh, obtained leave of the King to beat up
the Drum in London for voluntaryes, and had many that went over
to serve them, and the 4th September Shertogenbosch was yeelded
up unto the Hollanders.

9 August 1629
This day my unkle John Mounsell came into England, and staid
here till 6 March.

The 26th hereof my brother mr William Parkins was maried.

6 September
This day the Kings of England and france sware unto the articles of
peace, at Windesore, and at Paris: Sir Thomas Edmondes being extraordinary embassador in France, and Monsieur despreaux in
England. This peace was somewhat shaken by the taking of the
French plantation at Canada by Captaine Kerkes, who left there
150 men well fortifyed.

6 October
This day our new Charter was published by which the King made a
Maior, Aldermen etc, and a Governour of freemen in Dorchester.
And The same day all officers were chosen as followeth.[11]
    John Perkins, Maior.
Bailives.   Assistants.
    William Jolliff.   John Cooke.
    William Derby.   Joseph Paty.
Governour.   Henry Derby.
    John Long.   Richard Bury.

Constables.	Shreive of Dorset.
Richard Bury.	Angel Grey Esquire.
Christopher Wey.	Undersheriffe.
Ralph Perryn.	Robert Goldsborough.

29 October
This day John Parkins the younger was born, about 5 in the morning.

30 October
This day Mr Hollis was set at liberty after eight moneths imprisonment upon suretys for the good behaviour.

The same day Densell Hollis Esquire was set at liberty having laine 8 moneths prisoner in the Tower about some passages in the last Parlament. He was delivered upon his sureties for the good behaviour: but that Recognisance was shortly after yeelded up.

1 November
This day mr Henry Blachford was maried, and the last of this moneth mr Frederick Losse was maried.

5 November
This day the Earles of Bedford, Clare, and Somerset, and Sir Robert Cotton were confined and imprisoned at severall Bishops houses in London for reading and publishing a pamphlet, wherein was set out how the King and Counsell laboured to bring in the Excise of Holland, but not long after they were released, and within a moneth, admitted to kiss the Kings hand.

10 December
This day my sister Walker died of a Consumption and 22th November past Mrs Savidge widow died also.

23 December
This day Mr John Hill, Mr William Derby and Mr John Blachford rode to London in the behalfe of the Towne, to procure from my Lord of Suffolke, or from the Counsell, liberty to muster our men in the towne and to have a Captaine of our owne. The Earle of Suffolk referred it to his Lieutenants Deputys: and they shewed so

[107]

much coldness and unwillingness in it, especially Sir Thomas freke, that it came to nothing.

29 December
This day the towne bestowed upon Mr Hollis a standing cup of plate, which cost 20 marks, for his service done the Last Parliament.

1630

1 January 1629/30
This day after much expectation, Don Carlo Coloma came to London Embassador from the King of Spaine, and was brought over from Dunkerk in the Kings ships: Sir Francis Cottington being gon Embassador for Spaine about a moneth before. Don Carlo had audience at Whitehall the 6th January, where he motioned a treaty of peace. By the way, it is to be knowne, that the Spaniards lately sought peace of the Hollanders, but they refused to make any.

6 January
This day the Earle of Holland was made Lord Admirall, as was reported, but it was not so.

26 January
This night there were strange flashes of light seene in the sky, and the like on the 22 february, which much troubled the King and the Court. And the 11 february there was an earthquak perceived at the new Brewhouse.

12 February
This day Mr Hollis and the other Gentlemen of the Parlement were fined in the Star chamber for their caridge at the dissolution thereof, Mr Hollis 1000 markes, Sir John Elliot 2000 and so all the rest more or less. Mr Long was fined at £2000 and sent to the Fleete, for leaving his County, and coming to the Parlement while he was Sheriff of Wiltes.

1 March
This day was our Assises held here before Sir Thomas Richardson, Lord cheife Justice and Sir John Denham, Baron of the exchequer. None were executed. But at Winchester Mr Henry Dorington was condemned and hanged for killing his owne mother the Lady Dorington, in a barbarous maner. Mr Cross preached here at our Assises.

About this time came over a liger Embassadour out of France

[109]

and with him 12 Capuchins to live about the Queene, who was at this time great with Child.

21 March
This day about 9 a clocke in the evening, my Cousin Jane Bateman died at London.

10 Aprill
This day died William Earle of Pembroke suddenly at london, to the great astonishment of the Court. And in his roome Dr Laud Bishop of London was within 2 daies after by secret practises chosen Chancellour of Oxford.

At the same time there died the Earles of Shrewsbury and Sussex, and Anglesey, and the Lord Wotton: and so being 3 knights of the garters places void they were bestowed upon Sir Richard Weston, Lord Treasurer, The Earle of Lindsey, Lord high Chamberlaine, and the Earle of Exeter.

At this time the sickeness began to increase in London, and Cambridge and some other places thereabouts, caused, as men suppose, by the unseasonablness of the last winter, in which we had excessive raines, and no frost nor cold at all. It continued in London all the yeare, and yet never exceeded the number of 77 in one weeke.

About this time Wheate rose from 4s to 6s 8d the Bushell in our market, but afterwards it fell againe. Barley and oates were very deare.

The beginning of this moneth, many of this towne went to plant in New England and among the rest, mrs Sandford.

21 April
This day my father was sworne a justice of the peace for the Towne.

22 April
This day Mr Bourd maried Hester Bond.

About this time came certaine newes that the Hollanders had taken Fernambuco the cheife towne of Brasill, upon which they made great triumphs in Holland.

29 April
This day mr William Coker returned to live at Maypowder.

1630

17 May

This day there was a great uprore at Caen made upon mr Richard Samborne by the common people, because he transported Corne, in which his house was ruined, and himselfe in great danger.

20 May

This day my brother Walker was maried to his second wife, the daughter of Mr Cotton minister.

29 May

This day Prince Charles was borne, and baptised after the English maner the 27 of June. His Godfathers were the King of France, the Palsgrave, and the Godmother, was the Queene Mother of France. Their Deputyes were the young Duke of Lennox, the Marquis Hammelton, and the Dutchess of Richmond. His nurse is Mrs Windham daughter to mr Hugh Pine. Upon the birth of this Prince, there was a generall pardon granted, and the King came publikly to Pauls cross to give thankes unto god. A STAR APPEARED.

1 June

This day was a privat fast kept by certaine persons, for the turning away of the danger threatned, namely the remooving of Mr White.

10 June

Pezo 192li. sottile 1631 – 196

13 June

This day my unkle Mr John Gould died, and in his place of the 15 was chosen upon the 4th October, mr William Perkins, and for a Feoffee of Trinity his son James.

The 19th hereof Sir francis Ashley pleaded his owne cause in Star chamber, being endited of a conspiracy against Sir Thomas Coventry Lord Keeper, as that he showld scandalize him in saying he had taken a bribe of £600. He was acquitted by the vote of the table.

5 July

This day the poppet players craved leave to play here in this towne, and had a warrant under the Kings hand, yet were refused.

8 July
This day our Assises were holden before Lord Cheif Justice
Richardson, and Baron Denham. Mr Guy preached, no man exe-
cuted.

14 July
This day I was chosen Towne Steward.

20 July
This day Richard Hill maried Sarah Davidge. The 29th dicto
Stephen Thorlton maried Judith Miller, and 3 August, William
Haselbury maried Ann Bonger. And 14th September, Richard
Churchell was maried to Edith Blachford.

25 July
This day was made a Collection for Cambridge where the plague
continued very hot, there was collected and sent them £23.

August
Towards harvest Corne began to grow very deare, wheate was
worth 6s and 7s a Bushell, and so other grayn. Malting was restrained.

11 August
This day Thomas Warren pluckt downe a Stag at Mandbury.

18 August
This day we rode to the Court at Beaulieu, to procure the Kings letters to his Embassadors in france about our goods that was burnt
and spoiled at Rouen, and had them.

25 August
This day Joseph Purchase his man Davis fell upon a Corne pike and
died suddenly.

15 September
This day the Commissioners sate here about compounding with all
that had £40 Land or freehold, for their Knighthood, a course
which by the advise of the Lord Treasurer was taken over the whole
Kingdome, but it raised little money for most men made excuses.

4 October

Shereffe of Dorset.	Governour.
Sir John Meller.	Mr John Cooke.
Undersheriff.	Assistants.
Henry Arnold Junior.	Joseph Underwood.
Maior of Dorchester.	Henry Maber.
Richard Blachford.	Matthew Butler.
Bailiffs.	George Munden.
Mr Denis Bond.	Constables.
Mr Richard Savidge.	Richard Williams.
	John Roberts.
	Thomas Hiat.

9 October
By reason of the pestilence which continued in London, the Terme was adjourned from this day to the 27 dicto.

8 November
This time corne grew very deare, wheat was sold in our market for 8s the bushell, and in other townes of this county for 10s and in the North country far dearer, by meanes of the last wet winter. Wherupon there were Commissions sent downe to the Justices to command all men to bring to the Markets a certain quantity. In this towne Mr Maior bought up corne, and sold it to the poore at 6s 8d.

10 November
This day Dr Leighton escaped out of the fleete, where he was prisoner for a book which he wrote against the Bishops, calld Sions plea against the Prelacy. But he was taken againe, degraded, put in pillory at Westminster, had his nose slit, his eares cut of, and was branded in both cheeks with S, all which he endured patiently.

Death of severall persons.
> Thomas Sparrow 28 September.
> Old John Palmer 17 November.
> Sir John Walter, Lord cheif Baron 20th dicto.
> Old mr Carter of Pounall 21th dicto.
> Sir George Trenchard 25 dicto.
> The Lady Acland the 30 dicto.
> Mrs Joan Gould widow 9 december.

[113]

5 December
This day the peace with Spaine was proclaimed at London by the Heralds of armes, by which all prises taken within 14 daies after, were to be lawfull. Sir francis Cottingten was the man that lay in Spaine to conclude it.

6 December
This day at 9 a clocke in the evening My 3rd daughter was borne and baptised Marya secunda. Her sureties were, mr George Bull, mrs Rachell Parkins, and mrs Sarah Hill. She died the 5 January next. [? ho. 9 ant.]

9 December
This day the parsonage of Beere and Seton was bought and paid for by this towne and other well affected persons. It is valued at £120 per annum. It cost £1400 and is to goe to the maintenance of the ministers in this towne.
   About this time died many as.
            Edward Lord Conwey.
            The Lord Vicount Grandison.
            The Earle of Exeter.
            The Earle of Kelly.
            The old Countess of Barkeshire.
            Mr John Small of Melcombe 17 dicto.
            Mr Edward Clarke of Tanton 31th.
            His wife the 19th dicto.
            Young Mr Densell Hollis 27th.
            Old mr Jefferis of Weeke 30th.

15 December
Mr John Browne remooved from Dorchester to dwell at Frampton.

17 December
This day mr Robert Blake was arrested for debt, having gotten into his hands of diverse men £5000.

1631

7 February 1630/1
This day Mr William Perkins my brother died, and mr John Long succeeded him in place of a Capitall Burges: his wife was delivered of a Daughter called Mary the 24th of the same moneth.

The same 7th of February, I rode to London, and my Brother Samuel Whiteway went for Cambridge and was placed in Catherine Hall. My sister Mary went to sojourne in London.

22 February
This day Mrs Grace Browne was maried to John Stephens of Glocestershire, Counsellor at Law.

5 March
This day Sir francis Cottington landed at Weymouth coming out of Spaine, where he had beene to conclude the peace, and brought with him a great summ of money to be coined here, and returned over to Brussells for the King of Spaine.

10 March
This day were our Assises before Judges Richardson and Denham. Mr Ironside preached. None suffered death.

11 March
This day died Thomas Eyres. Sir John Cooper Baronet died 18 ditto. Mr William Bury 22th dicto. Mrs Rachell Underwood 18 Aprill. William Mundins wife 21 dicto. Mr George Browne of Tanton 22th dicto.

All this winter and the Spring Corne continued deere, both in England, and in most part of Christendome. In London it was worth 14s a bushell, in some markets about us 10s, in Bourdeaux ten crownes a Busshell. The Malters were restrained from buying barley or making any malt.

1 Aprill 1631
This day there was a solemne generall privat fast kept for the good

success of the King of Sweden, who went on very prosperously in his warrs, and had taken in all Pomerania, and Meckelburg, except one Towne.

6 April
This day the 2 Lord Cheife Justices and Baron Denham, tried the Earle of Castlehaven at Salisbury by a speciall Commission, and found him guilty of Sodomy, and of aiding Skypwith his Ganymede to ravish his owne Lady and his sons wife. The 25 he was condemned at Westminster by Sir Thomas Coventry, Lord high Steward and 27 Barons, and beheaded upon Tower Hill the 14th May 1631.

20 Aprill
This day the Justices sate the second time at Sherborne about the making of composition for Knighthood, for which all that had £40 land or freehold were brought in and made to pay the value of 3 subsidies.

22 May
This day Mr ferdinand Nichols was maried, and the 26th Mr Stephen Charlton was maried to my Cosen Elisabeth Middelton.

At this time came the newes of the King of Swedens prosperous success, who had taken all Pomerania and many other good townes, as Francfort upon the Oder from the Imperialists, and marched from thence into Silesia: as also of the resolution of all the Protestant Princes met at Leipsich to stand up for the liberty of Germany. But at the same time Tilly tooke Magdenburg, with very great slaughter of the inhabitants.

At this time the Prince of Orange went into the field with a great army, and sate downe before Bruges, but staid not there, but removed into Holland.

At this time the Countrey was full of reports of Captaine Skimmerton, who with a great nomber of people levelled all the enclosures in the forest of Deane and Braidon forest in Wilshire.

In this moneth died Dr Harsnet Arch Bishop of Yorke, Dr Buckridge Bishop of Ele, and Mr Walter Newburgh Minister of Simondsbury. They were succeeded by Dr Neale, Dr francis White, and Mr Glenham.

1631

The 21th dicto Mr ferdinand Nichols was maried, and the 6th June Mr Marshall maried with Mrs Whitefield.

17 June
This day I bought my blacke nag [?Lamb] at Yevell, aged 5 yeares.

18 June
This day and a good while after the drum was beaten here and elswhere to raise Voluntaries for the King of Sweden, who had 3000 out of Scotland, and as many out of England, conducted by the Marquis Hamelton, who departed 5 July.

This day Dr Wright Bishop of Bristoll came hither, and preached the 19th and visited the 20th.

12 July
κλᾶρα δακτυλῶν [? *Clara of fingers*][12]

14 July
Captaine William Simpson of Weymouth died suddenly, of an impostume broken within him, as it is conceived.

21 July
This day the Assises were held here before Cheife Justice Richardson, and Baron Denham. Mr Wake of Bincome preached: 6 were executed, and amongst them a maide of Weymouth for killing her child. Note that this last Trinity Terme, Lord Cheife Justice Richardson fell downe suddenly in the Court in Wesminster hall, of an convulsion, and was hardly recovered. Yet he came the Circuit, and at Salisbury a highway robber being by him condemned, threw a flint at him as he sate upon the bench, and strooke of his cap for which he had his right hand cut of presently, and soone after was hanged.

Death of diverse persons.
Dr Barlow Deane of Wells 21 July.
Sir Thomas Middelton senior 12 August.
Mr Matthias Nicols 15 dicto.
Mr Morton drownd at Blandford 17 ditto.
Lord Cheife Justice Hide 26 dicto.
Mr Robert Williams 5 September.
Mr James Frampton 6 September.

[117]

August
Dr Warburton was chosen Deane of Wells in Dr Barlows Rome,
and Lord Cheif Baron Damport made Lord Cheif Justice, and
Baron weston made Lord Cheif Baron, and Sir Richard Sheldon
made a Baron of the Exchequer, and Sir John Finch made the
Kings solliciter.

Mr Gardner troubled divers marchants to goe to London to be
examined before the Kings atturney about stealing of Custome the
last winter.

16 September
This day the matter was debated betweene the Capitall Burgesses
of this towne, and some discontented persons of the same, who
complayned of them that they had wronged them in procuring the
Charter, and not giving the Common Counsell power to chuse
their owne members. And this was clearly disprooved by Mr
Derby against Mr John Coke and Mr Joseph Paty who were their
speakers. Another complaint they made about the free Schoole,
which they said should be free for all, wheras the deed being pro-
duced, shewed that the Founder meant it should be free onely for
poore mens children. Sir francis Ashley was present at the debate,
and shewed them their errours, yet they went away unmanerly and
in an insolent maner cried out, a free schoole, a free schole. The
cheife of this faction were mr John Coke, Joseph Paty, George
Mundin, John Stevens, Thomas Whittell, William Mundin, Edward Brag, and old mr Vawter the instigator of all. Mr William
Savidge their Counseller, Dr Bradish and Mr Ironside their divines. The same men caried themselves tumultuously in the choise
of the Governor and Assistants the next Law day.

3 October
Maior of Dorchester was
chosen.
  Mr William Whiteway
    Senior.
Bailiffs.
  Mr John Hill 2.
  Mr James Gould 2.
Governour.
  Mr Joseph Paty.

Assistants.
  Mr John Coke.
  George Mundin.
  John Stephens.
  Thomas Whittell.
Constables.
  Thomas Hiat.
  Henry Sims.
  John Bushrod.

Sheriffe of dorset.   Undersheriff.
Brewen Williams Esquier.   Richard Talbot.

9 October

At this time came the newes of the great battell of Leipsich, in which the King of Sweden and the Duke of Saxony overthrew Tilly and all his army, slew above 20000 of them and Tilly amongst the rest. This battell was fought the 7th September old Stile. And the 11th of the Same moneth the Hollanders obtained a great victory over the Spaniards in Princeland. Then the King of Sweden came downe through all Germany, took in Erfurt, Hanau, francfurd etc.

The Duk of Saxonys forces under the Earle of Thurn took in Prague and all Bohemia. Marquis Hamelton, and Generall Horne overran Silesia.

21 October

This day the Portugall pirats that robed a french man upon this Coast was arrained at Weymouth, by a speciall Commission granted to Mr Maior, Mr Napper Vice admirall, Sir Nathaniel Napper, Mr Swaine Judge, and Mr Brewen Williams. 60 of them were condemned, but wer all pardoned except one Englishman, and one Irishman.

Death of severall persons.

Mr Adam Reve the 11th October.
My Son John the 2nd and 3rd Son 16 dicto.
George Mundins wife 31 dicto.
Mrs Walker of Cliff 13th November.
Sir Henage finch, Recorder, London 6 December.
Sir Hugh Middelton 7 December.

2 November. This day I ended the translation of Daubignés history.

4 November

This day the Lady Mary the Kings eldest daughter was borne at St James. The Earle of Carlile was Godfather, the Countesses of Dorset and Rocksborough were Godmothers.

5 November

This day the Duke of Vendosme came into England with a great traine.

31 November
This day mr John Nicolas Ruliss went hence to london to dwell, there having beene much stir about his departure.

5 December
This day was there made a solemne Pacification between the 15 of this town and the Commons, as they call themselves. Every man stressing his readyness, except mr John Coke, Patroclus Coke, and Roger Stephens. This was brought to pass by Mr Whites mediation.

Mr Littleton the Counsellor was chosen Recorder of london in Sir Henage finch his place. Sir Thomas Richardson was made Cheife Justice of the Kings bench, Sir Robert Heath made Ch[ief] Justice of Common pleas. Mr William Noy was made Atturney Generall against his will.

28 December
Clara Triandra nata A[nn]o 1593 [*Clara, who has had three husbands, born in the year* 1593][13]

The 27th of this moneth Mr William Derby of Dorchester mercer was maried, and the 19 January next, Mr Haidon was maried to my Cousin Elisabeth Gould of Haies neare Exon.

1632

24 January 163 1/2
This day there was a mighty tempest at weymouth with thunder and lightning. 8 men were dangerously hurt with it in the Pilgrim, and 2 slaine. It was terrible also in other places.

> Cousin Christiane Bateman died 12th dicto.
> Old Mrs Pelham of Compton 15 dicto.
> Dr Housdon Bishop Durham 5 february.
> John Williams of Heriston 6 february.
> Dudley Viscont Dorchester 18 Dicto.
> Unkle William Mounsell 1 March.
> Mrs Bond of Purbeck 17th dicto.
> Mr John Mellege of Poole 19 dicto.

This last man enjoined his executors to bury him in the finest holland, and to wrap his corps in the best crimson plush that could be got.

15 february
This day Mr fisher and Mr Haack departed hence to returne into Germany, but Mr fisher fell very sick at London of the stone, wher he lay long. And the 6 March Mr Schloer went also for the low Countries to live with Colonel Harwood as his Chaplaine.

10 March
This day my wife had a mischance, and a long weakeness after it.
    The Assises were held here the 1 of this moneth before Lord Cheife Justice Richardson and Baron Denham. Mr Hussey of Wolton preached. Mrs Jane Penny was here acquitted of the murder of a child which was laid to her charge with strong presumptions.

26 March 1632
This day my father Parkins had his gray gelding of £20 stolen by night out of his stable, but he had newes of him againe at Bristoll within 5 daies.

1 Aprill
This day Dr Buts Vicechancellour of Cambridge, hanged himselfe
in his chamber with a Towell: it is said, out of discontent, because
the king shewed much dislike at a play, which he had caused lately
to be acted before him in Cambridge, full of scurrility against the
gravest ministers of the Kingdome, whome they call Puritans.
Neare about the same time many in London and thereabouts de-
stroied themselves and others in a very fearfull maner.

6 April
This day the Kings of Sweden and Bohemia having Passed the
Danou, passed the Leck also and beate Tilly out of his trenches and
slew many thousands of his men, and by the victory made himselfe
maister of all Swevia and Bavaria, tooke in Augsburg and all the
great townes thereabout. This was done at Rain in Bavaria.

The 5 of this moneth the Archdeacon visited and Mr Sachevirell
preached.

The 10th hereof Gifford Bale maried Joane Davidge.

13 Aprill
This day the tide flowed twice in an hower at London bridge, which
was by diverse curiously observed as a Prognostick.

The 10th of this moneth, John Ward went into france, and my
brother John Whiteway came to live with mee.

May
This moneth there was a great lumpe of Ambergreece found on
the sea shore in Devonsheere, weighing 200lb which the King
seised on by his Commissioners, and gave him that found it a pension of £50 per Annum.

15 May
This day the Prince of orange tooke the feeld, beseeged Mastrickt,
which Pappenheim came to releive, but was beaten away with the
loss of 2000. At length after 3 moneths seige the Prince tooke it by
composition. There were many brave souldiers slaine before it, the
cheif were Grave Earnest of Nassau, the Earle of Oxford, and

1632

Colonel Harwood. From there the Prince went and took Limburg.

This Somer also County Henry Vanden Berg revolted from the Spaniards.

24 May
This day there was another company tried at Weymouth for piracy by an extraordinary Commission granted to Sir francis Ashley, Sir Thomas Trenchard, Sir Nathaniel Napper, John Browne Esquire and others. The Captaine was condemned, and repreived: He was a Portugall.

1 June
This day mr Thomas Blachford caried his wife and her Sister into france.

5 June
Mr William Derby was deputed by the marchants of this towne, to treate with the rest of the Marchants at London by order from the privy Counsell: about cutting of the processe of Marteau and Launay, and settling the french trade. To which purpose there was levied 12 per pound of the Custome paid for all goods caried to and brought out of france.

8 June
Upon the remoovall of mr Nathaniel Bernard Usher, Mr Nathaniel Cooke succeeded him in that place.

This Sommer mr Noy the Kings Atturney calld in question all Cottages upon the Statute, and drew in all the great houses about London upon the same.

28 June
Mr Luttrell came from Sidling to live here in this Towne.

5 July
Upon the remoovall of Mr Ruliss the place having beene a while supplied by mr Roger Derby, Mr John Strickland came to be mr Whites assistant: the towne promised him £50 per annum from Seton and mr White £30 more.

[123]

12 July
This day the Assises were holden here before Cheife Justice Richardson, and Baron Denham. Mr filer preached. 6 were put to death.

14 July
This day seven men were drowned in a boate betweene Poole and Sandwich in a storme.

25 July
Mr John Holles 3rd son to Densell Hollis Esquier was borne.

2 August
This day Mr Richard Bateman maried his 2nd wife, having beene a widow some 6 moneths.

4 August
This day the King came in his progress to Sarum, where he staied 3 daies and went from thence to Beauly.

31 August. This day John Bushrod was borne.
    The death of sondry persons.
            Sigismund 3rd, King of Poland 3 April.
            farmer Coward 11 May.
            Sir Ishaac Wake 27 May.
            Mr William Laurences wife 29 dicto.
            William Earle of Banbury 4 June.
            Mr John Adin 13 dicto.
            Justice Whitlocke 15 dicto.
            Philip Nicols 18 dicto.
            Parson Bartlet Monkton 19th dicto.
            Margaret Dashwood 21 August.
            francis Countess of Somerset died 24th.
            Mr John Gallot died 15 September.

2 September. This day the great house at Waterston was burnt.

10 September
William Mundin maried Thomasin foxwell, and 19th of the same Samuel Huet maried Anne Simmes. October 8 Mr Richard Blake

of Andover maried with Jane Dashwood, and 5 November Hugh
Philips maried Mary foxwell.

This day George Lord Digby, eldest son to the Earle of Bristell
Brought home his wife the Earle of Bedfords daughter which he
had lately maried. Ther came with him the Earles of Bedford,
Essex and Harford with their Ladies, and many other Lords, and
Lay at Sherborne lodge ten daies.

27 September
This day Mr George Hodder coming from Bridport Sessions fell
from his horse upon the way, and died Suddenly. More there died
about this time. The old Lady Meller widow to Sir Robert Meller
died 11 October. Old Mr Neuburgh 20th October. Mr Sutton of
Blandford a great learned man 25th October.

About this time the Marquis Hamelton returned out of Germany.

1 October
This day Mr Edmund Dashwood was chosen Maior of Dorchester.

Bailiffs.	Assistants.
Mr John Blachford 2.	Mr Joseph Paty.
Mr John Long.	Richard Bury.
Constables.	Edward dashwood.
John Bushrod.	Robert Napper.
Thomas Symonds.	Sheriffe of Dorsett.
Edward Brag.	John Browne, Esquire.
Gouvernour.	Undersheriff.
Mr Henry Maber. ·	Thomas Devenish.

12 November
John Lord Paulet of Hinton came with his family to live at Stinsford
for a while, out of his love to the hunting of the hare, which he much
affects, and in which this countrey excells.

About this time the French King obtained a great victory in Languedoc, against the Duke of Orleans and his party, in which the Duke
of Montmorency was hurt and taken prisoner, and afterwards with
many other great men beheaded at Tholousa. Monsieur was reconciled, but presently after he fell of againe. The Protestants refusing
to take part with him, were much graced for their fidelity.

6 November

This day the second battell of Leipsich was fought, betweene the King of Sweden on the one part, and the Duke of fridland for the Emperour on the other. The King of Sweden was slain in the field yet his men got the victory, and slew 6000 of the enemies. Papenheim was shot in pieces with a Canon, and fridland so wounded, that he died 3 weekes after. Duke Bernard of Saxen Weimar pursued the victory. Upon the King of Swedens death the Protestant Princes, appointed a meeting at Hailbrun, to consult about the prosecution of the warre. 13 daies after this battell, frederick King of Bohemia died at Ments.

2 December

This day King Charles fell sicke of the small pox, but by Gods mercy he soone recovered againe.

The 7 of this moneth the Lord Evers was sent to the Tower upon a writ of rebellion graunted out of the Chancery.

This winter season was very unhealthy by reason of the excessive raines all the Autumne and winter, and little frosts. In this towne, and the Countrey round about, there died a great nomber, and the report went about the Countrey that they died of the plague. There died about this time among others these persons of note.

Death of notable persons.

> Henry Earle of Northumberland 10 November.
> Sir John Elliot in the Tower 11 November.
> francis Earle of Rutland 30 November.
> John Holles Esquire a child 12 December.
> Mr John Long Bailiff 20 december.
> John Cob, Smith 31 december.
> Mr Gray of Kingston 6 January.

This John Cob died suddenly as he was ringing of a bell.

About the end of this moneth, the Earle of Arundell, the Lord Martravers and his Lady, the Earle of Dorset with many other Lords and Ladies were sent to the Hague to bring over the Queen of Bohemia with her younger children into England, and to treate with the States about the hering fishing on the coast of England: for which they agreed to pay £100000 for what was past and 2000 per annum for future time.

2 January 1632/3
This day mr Richard Bury was chosen a Capitall Burgess in the place of Mr John Long late deceased, and in his place of Bailiffe, William Whiteway the younger succeded.

At this time Mr John Strickland Mr Whites Assistant was by Sir John Horner presented to the Parsonage of Puddimores Milton, which he accepted to preserve it from the Lapse: he remooved hence the 19th february. And the place was supplied a while by mr Jonathan Lawrence, and afterwards by mr Giles.

3 January
At this time my Mother had a very great sickenesse, but by gods blessing upon the endevours of Captaine Salleneuve she was well recovered againe.

The 7 of this moneth Gerard Napper Esquire was maried to one of the heires of Mr Cole of Pitmister in Somersett.

The 22th of this moneth there came out a Commission to collect money of all men of ability towards the repayring of St Pauls Church in London: to which the king and many great men about London had given largely.
   This towne gave about £10 towards it. Sir Thomas Trenchard, and Dr Whetcome were commissioners for this town, and Dr Whetcome was very earnest.

26th The Round gold weights were stamped by Sir Thomas Ailesbury, who got a Patent for it from the King, with a Proclamation, that no other weights should be autheticall.

30th Mr Prin a Counsellor was sent to the Tower for writing a booke against stage plaies and dancing, which the Queene tooke to hart, because about the same time that his booke came forth, she acted her part in a Comedy before the King.

[127]

3 February
This day Mary Bull was Borne. Thomas Simonds borne 27 ditto.
Martha Patie borne 14 March.

6 February
Mr Shervill Recorder of Salisbury was fined £500 in the Star
Chamber for breaking a glass window of St Thomas Church in
Salisbury in which the Trinity was painted: which he might by his
office as Master of the Vestry have taken downe: but breaking it as
it stood with his staffe, he was censured. The Arch Bishop Neale,
and Bishop Lawd spake most bitterly against him, the Earle of Dorsett and Secretary Cooke were for him.

7 February
This day the King and Queene invited themselves to supper to Mr
Hugh Pery Sheriff of London, and went thither in great state,
which the Londoners much esteemed.

The 9 hereof Certaine Gentlemen that were made Feoffees for the
purchasing of Impropriations and settling of painfull ministrys
where they were most needfull, were censured in the Exchequer,
and the Parsonages they had purchased, adjudged to be in the
Kings guift.

11 February
This day a great part of London bridge was burnt, namely 43 faire
howses and in the fire perished 2 men, to the great losse of the
Chamber of the Citty.

13 February
The Citty of London was fined £1000 for the death of Dr Lambe,
who was killd in a tumult 4 yeares before, and paid it.

25 February
There was a warrant granted out for the apprehending of Mr John
Blachford and Mr Thomas Waltham, for refusing to answer to the
Information made in the Exchequer against them for stealing of
Custome, and counterfeiting of Cockets which was discovered by
Walter Gould who had beene their Cheife Agent therein. Where-
upon they absented themselves.

26 February
This day Christofer Gould maried with Rachell Beake, and shortly after, when Aquila Purchas, Bernard Gapen and others went for New England, he was by Mr White chosen Clarke of Trinitie Parish, and by the towne made Schoolemaister of Trinity schoole.

7 March
This day the Assises were held here before Sir Thomas Richardson Lord Chief Justice of Kings Bench and Sir John Denham Baron of Exchequer. Mr White preached. 3 persons were executed. And the Judges brought with them a Proclamation for prices of wine, Canary and Muscadi, and Alicant at 12d. Sack and Malaga at 9d and french wine at 6d. Rochell wine at 5d the Quart. Lord Richardson was sent for to the Court, before he had ended the Circuit.

21 March
There was a fire at Weymouth and Melcome Regis in which 2 houses were burnt, by the negligence of a Cooper, between Mr Henry Walthams and Mr Russells.
    Death of sundry persons.

> Mr John Bond of Purbeck 1 february.
> Matthew Chub 8 March.
> Little Thomas Simonds 12 ditto.
> George Gould 15 ditto.
> Captaine Colliers wife 16th ditto.
> Silvester Keech 18 ditto [?viste].

25 March 1633
Mr Robert Beake died this day. Mrs foxwell died the same day.
    Little John Bushrod 1 Aprilis. My Aunt Gould of Staverton 27 March. Mrs francis Clarke of Exon 2 April. Mrs Spicer widow 10th dicto.

Aprill 1. About this time the Earle of Holland sent a challenge to the Lord Weston eldest son to the Earle of Portland Lord Treasurer, for intercepting some letters of the Queenes and his directed to the Duke of Chevreuse, wherein they warned him to wake to himselfe, for he was in danger. These letters the Lord Weston intercepted as he returned home from his travells by sea and delivered them to the King, who opened them and shewd them to the Queene. Wherat she was greatly discontented. The King hearing of the challenge, confined the Earl of Holland to his house, and upon that the Queene tooke her bed in discontent and would not be spoken with. Many great persons also left the Court. But the busynes was shortly after reconciled by the King.

In this moneth of Aprill there were a great number of pilchards taken upon this coast, to the admiration of all men, who never knew any taken about this Season before.

12 Aprill
This day the new feoffement of the Lands of All Saints parish was sealed. The feoffees were mr Richard Blachford, mr Dionis Bond, mr James Gould, Mr John Blachford, William Whiteway Junior, Mr Richard Savidge, Matthew Buttler, Robert Lawrence, Edward Dashwood, and John Bushrod.

26 April
Philip Burlemacchi the great Marchant called beyond sea the Kings marchant, brak for £200000 and had a protection to keepe him from arrests.

28 April
The King was Godfather to the son of Sir William Balfoure Lieutenant of the Tower, and the same day released O-Rorck and the Lord Evers that were there prisoners. Mr Long and mr Prin were for that day sent to the fleete, and the next day returned to the Tower.

8 May
This day King Charles set forward in his Journey towards Scotland, attended with the Duke of Lenox, Marquis Hamelton, and 15 Earles, besides a great many others to the number of 4000 horse. He Came to Edinburgh the 14th June. The Queene in the Kings absence went and lay at Greenwich. The King was Crowned at Edinburgh and held a Parlement there, in which Lawde Bishop of london was made a Scotish lord and had voice; after some stay, the King came post to Greenwiche the 20th July and to london the 25th.

1633

This Easter Terme Sir Thomas Richardson Lord cheif Justice was fined £1500 for taking baile for the like somme due to the Bishop of Oxford after judgement, contrary to the Law.

This Easter Terme Dr Williams Bishop of Lincolne was questioned in the Star Chamber, for disclosing some of the Kings Counsell unto his Chancellor, of things passing while he was Lord Keeper.

Death of severall persons.

Mr Thomas Lockier of Waimouth 16 April.
Alderman Poole of London 19 April.
Petty a shoomaker kild himselfe 20th.
My sister Bushrod 21 Aprill.
Sir Thomas Freke going to london 5 May.
Dr Godwin, Bishop Hereford 6 May.
Mr Robert Girdler in london 16 May.
William Martin 25 May.
William Sims Smith 3 June.
Mr Allen parson of Abbotsbury 5 May.

This Mr Allen was drowned, as he was going into france, to fetch home Sir John Strangewaies his sons: having a little before married his sister Mrs Manning.

Sir John Bankes the Princes Atturney was made Lieutenant Deputy of Dorsett in the Roome of Sir Thomas freke, and Dr Juxton made Bishop of Hereford in steed of Godwin.

23 May
This day the Prince of orange after a moneths siege tooke Rheinberg. But the Spaniards affronting him with a great army, he could undertake no other enterprise this Somer.

22 June
Mr Thomas Newman, and mr Robert Angell came hither with their wives, and Cousin Peter middelton, and staid here one weeke.

Before the King went into Scotland, the Lord Keeper Sir Thomas Coventry had a warrant to seale a pardon for the forfeitures of the Papists, which he refusing to do, as contrary to Law, the King sent for him, called him his maister, and tooke away the Great Seale. But upon some words of the Earle of Dorsett, who said, he knew the King would not condemne any man without hearing him, they were restored unto him againe.

Whitsonales and May games were this yeare much countenanced by speciall order from the Court in which Sir Robert Philips and Sir Charles Barkley of Somersetshire were very forward. But Sir Arthur Hopton got a petition subscribed with the hands of 36 Justices of that County, to the which the 2 Knights aforesaid, and Dr Godwin refused to subscribe. This petition he presented to the King at Woodstocke, where the King conferred with him about it in privat, and gave him such satisfaction, that at his returne he bound over 120 of the Revellers unto the Assises. The sum of the petition was to set out the dangerous consequents of Whitsonales, in which severall murthers had beene this yeare committed in that same county.

27 June
Mr John Caspar Hopff was maried to his wife Catherine Gardener. 15 July William Miller Brewer was maried to Mr Sticklands daughter: and the 23 July Mr John Hardy was maried to Alice Toope.

29 June
This day the Landgrave of Hesse, and others won a notable victory at Hammellen against the Imperialists. Merude, Grunfeld, and Bonninghansel, routed their army slew 5000, tooke 1500 prisoners, and all their ordinance and cariages.

2 July
Mr Henry fisher went for Germany, and Mr Giles went away into Glocestershire to a living: and Mr Jonathan Lawrence assisted Mr White for a time.

5 July. Dr Gilbert Jones visited, Mr Tailor of Waimouth preached.

6 July
This day Thomas Lord Viscount wentworth set forward from london towards Ireland where he was to be Lord Deputy, accompanied with 100 coaches.

25 July
The Assises were held here before Lord cheife Justice Richardson, and Baron Denham. Mr Edward Pele preached. 4 offenders were executed.

1633

25 August
My unkle John Mounsell came to Minehead, after 4 yeares absence in Ireland.

28 August
My brother Joseph Parkins to prevent a consumption had an issue made in his arme by Captain Salleneuve. He died 26 October next.

29 August
Mr William Lawrence of Stepleton was maried unto mrs Margaret Cheek, widow.
  The death of severall persons.

> Elliot Johnson died at Poole 25 June.
> Mr Roberts of Poole died 26 June.
> Mr David Giare of Waymouth 28 ditto.
> Old mr Arundel of Chidioke 19 July.
> Mrs Penelope Trenchard of Warmwell dicto.
> Mr Sheldon brake his necke 23 ditto.
> Old Lady de la Warre died 25 ditto.
> Old Mr Robert White of Waimouth 27 ditto.
> Dr Abbot, Archbishop Canterbury 4 August.
> Young Countesse of Suffolke 21 ditto.

The Countesse of Suffolke was buried in great pompe at Audley end, and the Archbishop at Croidon. Dr Lawde Bishop london succeeded him in the Archbishoprick. And Dr Juxton elect Bishop of Hereford succeeded him in the Sea of London.

  A Gentleman went to Reading to see the house where Dr Lawde was borne, and seing the stocks, pillory, and whipping post stand before it, he noted it. The next weeke order was sent to the Maior of Reading to remoove them thence, and place them some where els. And in Michaelmas terme following, a Gentleman was fined £2000 for saying the ArchBishop was an Arminian.

2 September
Mr Gardener and mr Blachford had a commission at Waimouth about the Custome causes. Mr Blachfords commissioners were Mr Lawrence of Wraxall and parson Simons of Melbury. Mr Gardners were, Mr Robert Smart, and Mr Woolfreys of Hampton. Mr Gardner seing he could not proove things as he desired, snatcht up the

commission, and put it in his pocket, which Mr Blachford certified into the Exchecker.

11 September
This day my daughter Elenor was borne ½ houre after 2 a clocke in afternoone. The sureties were, Mr Dionis Bond, my Aunt Paty, and my sister Mary Whiteway. The Lord blesse her.

About this time the Lady Willoughby came and sent her husband Sir Robert Willoughby out of his estate and farme at Turnerspiddl, upon a grant made by the King, it being forfeited, and by her begd.

30 September
This day new officers were chosen for this Towne. viz.

Maior.	Governour.
Mr William Jolliffe.	Mr Edward Dashwood.
Bailiffs.	Assistants.
Mr William Derby 2.	Mr Henry Maber.
Mr Richard Bury.	Henry Derby.
Constables.	Joseph Underwood.
Mr Edward Brag.	John Bushrod.
Mr Robert Lawrence.	Sheriff of Dorset.
Mr Nicholas Stone.	William Collier Esquire.
	UnderSheriff.
	Matthew Derby.

This yeare also Sir John Meller was made Sheriff of Oxfordshire.

This day mrs Grace Trenchard was maried unto the son and heire of Sir John Pole Baronet: videlicet William Poole.

15 October
This day James Duke of yorke was borne, and baptised the 24 November. Upon his birth Mr Prin was released out of the Tower after 9 moneths imprisonment for writing a booke against playes and maskes, at which the Queene found her selfe agreeved.

The 16 hereof, Mr fitzherbert Archdeacon visited, Mr Bull of Purbeck preached. This day mr Charles Gagé a french Painter came and wrought in this towne, for 5 weekes. He drew my picture and my wives and many others.[14]

1633

18 October

The King set forth a booke, to give liberty unto sports and pastimes upon Sunday after Evening praier, in confirmation of the like liberty granted to Lancashiremen in his returne out of Scotland 1617. And required all ministers to publish it in the Church. Which diverse in conscience refused to do, and many after they had read it, shewed that it was against the word of God.

This yeare that part of fordington field that lies between frampton way and the River, was Enclosed and made a Cowlease and their Moore, which before was their Cowlease, was now turned into a Meadow and watered.

The 21 hereof My Lord Paulet, and Mr Rolles with their families came to Stinsford and lay there for hunting untill the 7 of December. The 29th November, the Duke Soubise came thither also, and went with them to Hinton.

The 26 October John Guppy was maried to Jane Melledge.

9 November

This day John Ward came from Mortain and returned thither 1 December.

The 23 of this moneth Mr Ignatius Jordan wrote to Dr Hall Bishop of Exon lying in London to moove the King for the calling in of his booke lately set out for sports upon Sundaies, or to shew his letter to the King, which he did, and wrote a sharpe letter backe to Mr Jordan, taxing him for his indiscreete zeale. The King was offended with his letter, because it seemed to call his Prerogative in question.

27 November

This day Patrike an Irish Jesuite was drawne hanged and quartered at Tiberne for a Traitor. His crime was this. Being in a Gentlemans company in Spaine, he sware he would never come into England, unlesse it were to kill the King. The same Gentleman met him afterwards in London, and tooke acquaintance of him, and after recalling his former words to mind, he revealed it to the Privy Counsell, whereupon he was apprehended, and condemned, and executed.

Sir Dominicke Sarsfield Viscount and Lord Cheife Justice of Ireland was fined in our Star Chamber £3000 to the King, and £2000 to the parties wronged, besides loss of his office and imprisonment during the Kings pleasure for putting one Bushy an Englishman unjustly to death in Ireland in his Circuit. He was sent prisoner to the fleete.

The lords of the Counsell sent to all Citties and Townes to have the Names of those that were thought fit to retaile Tobacco: and when their Names were returned up, they sent them downe licences to retaile it, forbidding all others to doe it.

16 December
There was another commission held here at the Shirehall, about Stealing of Customs. Mr Lawrence of Wraxall, and John Cole were for mr J. Blachford, and mr Robert Smart, for mr Gardner. It lasted a moneth.

This quarter died these persons.
> Henry Viscount faukland 28 September.
> Mr John Cooth 12 October.
> My Brother Joseph Perkins 26 October.
> Old Lady Thornix 15 November.
> The Archduchess, Infanta Isabella Clara
>   Eugenia died 1 December.
> Dr Arnesius died at Franiker in December.
> John Turbervile of Wooll died [*illegible*].

20 December
Mr Hugh Thompson, of Queenes College in Oxford, came to be Assistant to Mr White in the Ministery, and was to have £60 per Annum for his paines, with augmentation of maintenance, when his occasions require.

29 December
Mr Maior commanded the posts to be cut downe, which those of Fordington had sett up at the inner end of Nutmeg lane.

The 30 of this moneth the Mary of Morlaix laden with 120 fardles of derbys for Dorchester, Waymouth and Hampton was cast away upon Portland beech and all the goods. The men forsook the barke, when they might have saved her. The greatest losse fell upon mr John Blachford, mr James Gould, and mr Thomas Waltham.

31 December
There was an earthquake at Colliton, Seaton and Beere in Devonshire. And a little after the like in Lancashire, where a River was dried up, and brast out again.

1 January 1633/4

This winter Mr Forbes, a Scotishman, minister of the English Church at Delfft in Holland having beene sent for over by the King, returned backe into Holland. The King sent for him to employ him about the English discipline in the English Churches in the low Countreyes, which he flatly refused to doe, but said, he would hinder it to his power. Whereupon the King told him, that if hee would doe it, he would make him a Bishop, and he rejecting the offer, the King dismissed him of his Charge at Delfft, having power from the States to appoint Ministers and discipline for the English Churches there. In this conference Mr Forbes told the King, that King James a little before his death sent for him out of Holland, and told him very seriously, that he desired him to give him a Reason, why it came to pass, that he had found the Scotish Church good and left it bad, and that he found the English Church bad, and should leave it far worse. Forbes said it proceeded from the Bishops whose goverment was Antichristian. The King James craved his advise how it might be remedied: Forbes told him it might be easily altered in Scotland, where that Goverment was not yet to throughly settled, and in England also it might be done, so it were wisely managed. King James promised to thinke upon some course to effect it, and to advise farther with him about it: in the meane time he charged him to conceal this their conference. The next news that forbes heard of the King, was of his death: how [it] came God knowes.

28 Januuary

This day Joseph Underwood the younger was maried, and 6 february, the young widow Mrs Joane Chub, was maried in London to Mr Thomas Man.

3 February

This day the Gentlemen of the Ins of Court namely the 4 cheife houses, Inner and middle Temple, lincolnes and Grayes in, danced a maske before the King and Queene in the Banquetting house at Whitehall. Each house set forth 4 Revellers, and 25 Gentlemen Riders, who rode in great magnificence from Hatton house through the Strand. This maske cost the actors 17000 pound and did so please the King, that he invited himselfe, the Queene and Maskers to sup at the Lord Maiors, Sir Ralph freeman the 13 february. Where the Lord Maior spent £3000 to entertaine them, in pulling downe diverse houses between his house and Marchantailors Hall, and making a gallery for the King to pass through. The King invited himselfe to the Lord Maiors, to make him amends, for the sharpe words he had lately given him, calling him old foole, for speaking in the behalfe of the Sopeboilers and Laundresses of London. Which troubled him so that he kept his bed a whole moneth after it, and was like to dy, had not the Kings message revived him. The Queene dancing at the Lord Maiors, strained her foote and was like to have taken much hurt. This maske should have beene danced on Candlemas day which was Sunday, to countenance the Kings booke, but at the request of the Gentlemen of the Ins of Court, as it was thought, it was put off till Monday. The same night the King gave a banket unto all the maskers, and he and the Queene began to eate first, and they would not let any of the lords or ladies [t]ast it, till the Maskers had done. In this maske the Lady Pie had a foule affront put on her, being turned out by the Lord Chamberlaine, because her husband refused to let his son be one of the Maskers to save charges.

17 February
Mr William Prin Counsellor of law, having beene long imprisoned for a booke which he wrote against dancing, and masks and enterludes, was now censured in the Star chamber, fined £5000 to the King, to stand in pillory, loose his eares, to plead nor write no more. The aggravation of his offences, which the Atturney insisted upon was, that he had let fall some passages, which cast an aspertion upon the Queene.

19 February
This day Mr Hugh Thomson was promised £100 per annum, as long as he used his Ministry here, by mr Maior and the company. Whereupon he promised not to leave us to accept any other preferment.
 Proclamations and orders came forth from the King and Coun-

sell, to forbid all men to sell Tobacco without speciall licence, as also to regulate the prices of ordinaryes, Ins, Tavernes, Hosteries etc.

27 February
This day the Assises were held here before Sir Humfrey Damport Lord Cheife Baron, and Baron Denham. Mr Clement preached. One man was executed, for breaking the necke of a wench whome he had gotten with child at Bridport.

This month Mr Durans a Scottish Minister, having taken incredible pains with the King of Sweden, and all the Protestant Princes and States in Germany about the reconciling of the Calvinists and Lutherans, returned into England, and came to Dr Lawd Archbishop, to know what assistance or furtherance he might expect out of England for that weighty busyness. The Archbishop told him that it was a mystery of State, and that he durst not meddle in it: but offred him a good Parsonage in Cornewall, if he would accept it, and upon his acceptation, gave him letters of presentation thereunto. Durans went into Cornwall with his letters, and there found the Incumbent living and in good health, so was disappointed.

About this time one Browne a Master of Arts in Oxford in his sermon praied for the dead, and another in Cambridge maintained in his sermon Justificacion by workes, and neither of them was questioned for it.

Mrs Joane Chub a young widow was maried unto mr Thomas Man of london the 6 of this moneth.

The 15 of this moneth Walstein the Emperors Generall was by the Emperours Command Killed at Egra in Bohemia by one Gourdon a Scot, and Butler an Irishman, two Imperiall commanders, because he had plotted to fall from the Emperour, and to Joine with the Swedes. Shortly after Otto Rhingrave overthrew the Duke of Lorraine in a Battell, and tooke all his Ordinance and baggage, and many of his Commanders prisoners.

This moneth Sir Richard Saltonstall, mr John Humfreys, and others of the cheifest of the Newengland Planters, were sent for to the Counsell table, and were required. 1. to take the oath of Allegeance. 2. the oath of Supremacy. 3. to subscribe to the discipline of the Church of England. The two oaths they tooke, but refused to subscrib unto our discipline, saying they went unto New England principally to decline that. Whereupon after some consultation they were dismissed.

Robert Earle of Lindsey was made High Constable of England for a time, for the taking up of some controversyes that had happened between certain Gentlemen which had challenged the field. He had beene also high Constable three years since, to determin the accusation between the two Scots, Rey and Ramsey.

2 March
The wife of Thomas Galpen of this towne Killed her young child of ½ a yeare old, for which she was imprisoned, and afterwards executed to death at the Summer Assises, sentenced by Baron Denham.

4 March
King Charles fell from his horse at Newmarkett as he hunted, and bruised himselfe, but shortly after he recovered, and returned to Whitehall, to entertaine young Prince Oxesteyrne, the son of the Chancellor of Sweden, who came to London the 15 of this moneth, as Ambassadour from his father and the Princes of Germany. He was attended by 80 Lords, Commanders and Gentlemen, and had audience the 26 of this moneth, when he made a speech unto the King of three quarters of an houre, in Latin, and afterwards unto the Queene in french of a quarter of an houre. The summe of his Embassage was to demand of the King £50000 in mony, and a supply of 12000 men, to be paid by the Princes as soone as they were come into Germany, for the maintaining of the wars. His commission being questioned, he sent to the Diet at Franckfort, and had a new one from the Princes there. Yet his request was denied and he returned discontent 10 June.

The Great Turke disarmed the English and french, and Venetian Ambassadors at Constantinople, and drew great fines from them, from the English 36000 Rix dollars for fighting with his Galleys that set upon some English ships that caried away Corne for the Venetians. And from the french for bringing Tobacco into his dominions against his edict. These troubles made the Turky marchants of London forbeare to send any goods thither for 6 moneths, till some order might be taken to reconcile them.

9 March

After a long wet winter, whereby most of the sheepe in Somerset, and many in Dorset were coathed, this day the dry weather began, and never rained till the 9 Aprill. Corne was deare this yeare wheate worth 6[s] 8[d] Barley 4s.

14 March

This day Sir Ralfe Freeman Lord Maior of london died, and the next day Thomas Moulson Alderman was chosen in his roome, and 2 daies after was sworne in the Tower.

18 March

After many thousands spent in law, Mr Blachford and Mr Gardener referred their differences upon account unto mr John Lawrence, and mr Henry Cuttance, who sate on it this day, but could not agree, so the busyness was referred unto Sir John Strangewayes to be Umpier, who tooke time to deliberate on it, untill the 1 August.

19 March

Stephen Terry was maried to Mr John Hardeys sister, and Mr Andrew Chaldecote unto the daughter of Mr Southe. Joseph Underwood Junior was maried 28 January.

25 March 1634

       Mr Knot of Bridport died 6 January.
       Mr Sherfield, Recorder of Sarum 26 died.
       Mr Pope of Manston 12 february.
       Sir Thomas Crew died 22th february.
       Andrew Spratlin died 23 february.
       Thomas Reade died 6 March.
       Old Hugh Manuell died 7 March.
       Mr Thatchers wife died at Sarum 23th.
       Mr John Drake of Wareham died 25.
       Mrs Joan Waltham of Waimouth 28.
       Mr Christopher Earle died 29 March.

Mr Harbert of london was chosen Recorder of Salisbury in the place of Mr Sherfield.

26 March

This day my nephew George Bull was borne.

4 Aprill

This day Cousin John Harvey of Lime went to St Christofers Is-
land.

The 11 of this moneth mr Thomas Blachford being come into England about busyness was like to be betrayed into the hands of a Pursivant, by mr John Gardner, who had a quarrell at him for beating
him at Bolayes. But he escaped him, and lodged the night at mr
Knaptons, whose backe house was burnt the same night by the negligence of a servant, who let a snuffe fall among the Turves. William Burt Tailor was so affrighted with this fire, that he died within
10 dayes after.

This moneth the Lord Horace Vere obtained a dismission from
the States under whome he had beene a Colonell many yeares. His
old Regiment was distributed among other companies, and his
new Regiment given unto the Lord Gorings son. The States in
acknowledgement of his good service assured unto him a pension
of £30 per Moneth, during his life.

12 April

The wife of mr Matthias Nicols deceased came to live here in
towne, and the 16th Mr John Luttrell remooved hence to live in
Marshwood Vale.

About this time the King granted a Monopoly of Coaches in london, who for a sett fee, caried all passengers caried up and downe
london streetes, to the great vexation of the watermen, who many
times fell by the eares with these new Coachmen in the streetes.

15 April

Patroclus Cooke maried to his 2d wife.

17 April

Mr Neuburgh of Marshwood Vale and many others set saile from
Waimouth towards New England: and the 27 of the same Mr John
Humfreys with his wife the Lady Susan Fines, set saile likewise for
the same place. This Somer there went over to that plantation at the
least 20 saile of ships, and in them 2000 planters.

18 April

Mr George Lawrence his house was burnt at Steepleton.

May

Farthings were growne so many and so burdensome to the country, by meanes that such quantity were brought in out of Holland,
and many coined by Tinkers at home, that all that had not a double
circle about them, were forbidden by proclamation. Divers Coyn-
ers of them were apprehended and censured.

7 May

Mr Prins sentence was executed: he lost one eare at Westminster
this day, and the 10th dicto the other eare in Cheapside, where all
his bookes which could be had, were publikely burnt. He was
thence returned to the fleet, and afterwards to the Tower. He endured his mutilation with much courage. The Printer that printed
his Histriomastix was fined £500 and stood upon, but not in the pillory.

13 May

At Glastonbury, while the people were busy setting up of a
Maypole, it fell on the head of a son of one of the most forward as he
ran over the streete, and beate out his braines.

22 May

I rode with my wife to Sherborn, Castell Cary, Wells, Axbridge,
Bath, Binegar and Glaston, and Shapwicke, and returned home
the 4th June. In this journey I was in the Bath and heard Dr Perce
Bishop of Bath and wells, and Dr Rivet preach.

Captaine Robert Browne being fallen behind hand, went into
Ireland to settle there, and swimming his horse through a great
river oftentimes in a bravado, at the last he was drowned.

Cousin George Gould was born 6 dicto. Cousin Nathaniel Bond
born 14 June.

About this time Sir George Horsey sold Clifton, and all his land
thereabout unto Mr Hele of devon Esquier and had for it 28000
pound.

2 June

Mr Bernard Toope overruled by his wife went hence to live at Chaldon against his will. But at Michaelmas next he was chosen Maior,
and being invited home, he returned the week after his election.

7 June

William Browne bookebinder was maried to Ruth Melledge and
21 July George yeate was maried.

This moneth there were discovered some Gentlemen of the
Innes of Court and others, to have coined the value of £30000 in
20s pieces of gold, the borders gold and the midle of it copper. The
cheifest of them fled, and the rest that were taken, were executed.
Upon this followed the descry of all English gold in France, where
22s G past at 28s and 20s at 26s so that very great quantityes were
transported over by stealth. Alderman Ducys servant and Cashier
had a hand in this coining and suffred death for it, which brake his
Masters hart.

This moneth there came out of Spaine to London £80000 to be
new coined there, and made over to Brussells to pay the Spanish
souldiers. A course that hath been held ever since Endimion Porter
came out of Spaine. Our King hath proffitt by the coinage, and for
it the whole Court leanes much to the Spanish party.

21 June

Sir Thomas Trenchard returned from London, where he and all
his houshold had laine 3 moneths for the curing of an impostume
in his necke.

22 June

Richard Veale and his wife Mary bare penance openly for an
obscene abuse offred to Bucke of Fordington, who died shortly
after it. She had been a moneth in Bridewell for it, and was well
whipt there.

24 June

The Sommer was very dry, and great scarcity of grass in dry
grounds: and so it continued till neare Christmas. About All Saints
water was scarce in many places.

At this time Mr Henry Derby remooved hence to live at Beaminster.

There were a great many notorious witches discovered in Lancashire this yeare and many of them hanged. Some of the cheifest
were brought to London, to satisfy the curiosity of the King and
Queene, who desired to see them play some of their feates.

William Burt Tailour died Aprill 21.
Joseph Cuffe died at Stockbridge 19th dicto.
Dr Bowle, Bishop of Rochester 24 dicto.
John Martin of Melcom drowned 30 Aprill.
My Grandame Parkins died 10 May.
Lady Jane Browne died 11 May.
Robert Brown Captain drowned 16 May.
My Grandsire W. Perkins died 17 May.
Cousin Debora Meech died suddenly 11 June.
Sir Edward Coke, late Lord Cheife Justice died 12 June.
Edward Doule Pavier died 23 June.
Mrs Uroth Allimbrig died 7 July.

3 July
This day Sir William van Ensam, one of the States of Hollands sons, with his tutour Johanes Van Schulenbrouck came to live here. They lodged at mr John Blachfords and dined at Mr Whites.

July 3 there were 4 small thatcht houses burnt at the east side of the South Gate of this towne, by the negligence of Parkes his wife. A collection was made for them in our 3 churches, in which there was £22 9s collected and distributed amongst them.

This Sommer Sir Walter Earle made a Decoy poole in his heath at Moordon in imitation of that in Rodney Stoke in the County of Somersett, where every yeare they take so much wildfoule as is worth £300 per annum. The inventer and keeper is a dutchman.

This yeare the King and Queen went their progress Northwards into Yorkeshire and Nottinghamshire, to hunt in Sherwood forrest.

The 7 of this moneth, mr Betscome having obtained licence of my Lord Keeper to yeeld up his place of Coroner, a new Coroner was chosen at the County Court, namely Mr Robert Rawe Gentleman. A greater number of freeholders came in afterwards and chose Mr John Michell, but the first election stood, by the appointment of the Judges at the next Assises.

The reading of the Kings booke for recreations upon Sunday was eagerly urged in Somersett by the Bishop of Bath and wells, and in the diocess of Winchester, and diverse ministers suspended for refusing to reade it. They all appealed from the BB to the delegates. The Bishop of Bristoll and the Chancellor urged Mr White to read it before the Archbishops Visitation: and upon his refusall, the Churchwardens in his absence procured Mr Holliday to reade it on a friday morning 11 July, none being then at Church, but he and the Clarke and the Churchwardens. When Mr White heard of it he was exceeding angry. It was read in St Peters Church. Mr Ben refused utterly to reade it.

12 July
This Act. Cousin John Moris Canon of Christchurch proceeded Doctor of Divinity, and Cosen John Midelton Master of Arts in Oxon.

13 July
This day being Sunday a young man of Beaminster was killd by his fellow with a knife after he had been sporting and drinking all the day, against the will of his mother, who charged him to stay at home: his name was [*entry incomplete*]

The 15 of this moneth Sir Nathaniel Brent the Archbishops Vicar Generall, having visited all the west country, visited here the Deanery of Dorchester, and the next day, the peculiars of this County. The first day here preached Mr Moone of Maine, and taxed the Justices that punish ministers for going to the Tavernes. The 2 day preached Mr Pit an Arminian, and inveighed against the repeating of sermons. The Vicar lay all the Visitation and 3 daies before at Wolton at Sir Thomas Trenchards: he was feasted one night here by Mr Jolliffe Maior, at the charge of the Towne. He pressed upon the clergy, the observation of the ceremonys very earnestly, as bowing at the name of Jesus, the surplis, and the reading of double services with much more, affirming that the present Archbishop would require no more then hath been required ever since the Reformation. While he lay at Wolton, Sir Thomas Trenchard fell downe at the staires and was like to breake his necke.

17 July
This day the Assises were held here by Sir Humfry Damport, Lord Cheife Baron, and Sir John Denham Baron of Exchequer. There were 4 hanged, namely Galpens wife for killing her child, and one of them was caried to Poole and hanged there in chaines for killing

and cutting in pieces a maide to whome he was a suter. After he was condemned, he plotted to kill the hangman in the prison: Mr fuller preached, a man of admired memory.[15]

This moneth a Parlement was summoned at Dublin, and held before Vicount Wentworth, Lord Deputy, in great state. The conclusion of it was the granting of 6 Subsidies over all Ireland, payable in 3 yeares. And these were the 1 subsidies that ever that Kingdome paid.

22 July
This day Mary Parkins was sent to Salisbury, to schoole.

23 July
Cousin William Gould shooting London bridge, the boate was overturned, and two of his companions drowned. He was in great danger also himself.

This Somer the Earle of Holland being Cheife Justice in Eyre, held an extraordinary Sessions in Glocestershire, to enquire of wrongs done to the Kings forests in that quarter, and according as he found men had offended he imposed as many fines, as amounted unto £200000. Sir John finch did good service in this employment, for which he was afterwards rewarded with a Cheife Justices Places. The cheifest offenders were Mr Mynnes, Sir Basell Brok, Mr Gibbins etc. most of whome were Papists, and were thought to be busy in destroying the Kings woods, of purpose to weaken the Kingdome for shipping in time to come, and so to expose it the more easily to invasion.

This Somer Henry Browne of Bridport went and planted himselfe in Ireland.

30 July
Sir John Strangewaies after many delayes and much intreaty made an arbitration between Mr Blachford and Mr Gardner wherein he gave Mr Blachford the value of £250 from Mr Gardner who demanded of Mr Blachford £1100. The next day he made a declaration, wherein he showed that he had committed an error of £100 upon his Arbitration.

Mr Strong, a fellow of Catherine Hall in Cambridge, was accused by one of his companions for scandalous words spoken against the present Archbishop of Canterbury, and the late Archbishop of

[148]

yorke Harsnet: for which he resigned up his fellowship to the house, and another was chosen fellow. He shortly after maried a rich young widow in Cambridge, being employed by Mr Goodwin to court her for him and in November following, Mr Tutchin re-moovig to Charminster he was by mr Pele settled in the Vicaridge of Fordington.

1 August
Young Mr Fry of Culliton coming from Exon with his man, bet-ween them they Killd a man at Vinneton bridge. For which his man was burnt in the hand, and Mr Fry had a pardon.

2 August
There came some cheaters out of the North to buy wooll in this countrey, and with a Loadstone some got 6 or 7 pound in a weight. They deceived Mr Ironside of Steepleton and many others, till being discovered, they got it by going.

6 August
This yeare Mr White left of the celebrating of the Anniversary of the great fire, which happened anno 1613.

15 August
Mr John Nicolas Rulice came out of the Palatinat to london with let-ters to the King, for a collection for the restoring of the university of Heidelberg. But when matters succeeded ill in Germany, he pre-sented them not, but went a while after unto Amsterdam, to be Minister of the English Church there.

Mr William Noy the Kings Atturney died 10 August, and made a conceited will: Sir John Bankes succeeded him in his place. Sir Robert Heath, Ch[ief] Justice of the common pleas was put out, and Sir John Finch succeeded him. Sir Robert Heath upon petition to the King, by his leave pleaded againe, at the Barre. Mr Littleton was made the Kings Sollicitor and Mr Robert Mason Recorder of london by mediation of the Kings letters.

17 August
Two men being at bowles near to Bridport on a Sunday, one beat out his fellowes braines with a bowle.

26 August
This day the Imperialists won the famous battell of Nordlingen of the Swedes, and took Gustavus Horne prisoner. The Imperialistes were led by the King of Hungary and the Cardinal Infant of Spaine, who after this victory, went to Brussells, and was reteined Governour of the low Countreys for the King of Spaine.

29 August
This day the towne of Beere Regis was burnt the most part of it to the ground, with great quantity of Corne. The loss is valued at 20000 pound. The Countrey sent them in above £500 speedily to releive their presents wants. Dorchester sent them above £40.

8 September
The Ministers of Surrey that were questioned for refusing to reade the Kings booke for Sports on the sabbath day, were all restored from suspension except two, against whom the Chancellor had other matters.

9 September
The Earle of Pembroke and Mongomery feasted the Duchess of Buckingham with great magnificence at Wilton, a whole weeke, about the accomplish of the mariage between his Son and her daughter.

The King made a Monopoly of Sope, forbidding all other to be used, but such as was made by the Patentes, which was so filthy that men refused to use it, and the Patentees compounded with the Sope boilers of London, giving them leave to use their trade againe, allowing them 4d out of every Barrell of Soape.

17 September
Mr John James Treder a Gentleman of Pomerania, came to live here, and lay at Mr John Blachfords with Mr [Ensum].

24 September
Mr Giles Greene came out of Purbeck to live here in this town by occasion of his owne and his wives sicklynesse.

27 September
A cheating companion stood in Pillory, for abusing the countrey

[150]

with counterfeiting a Patent for marking of Cattell, which so terrifyed the common sort that some marked their Cattell all night,
others on Sundaies, and raisd up pitch to 16d the pound.

4 October
Mr Robert Tutchin remooved from fordington to live at Charmister, where Sir Thomas Trenchard gives him £40 per annum besides the house and garden in which he lives.

6 October
This day were chosen officers for Dorchester.

Maior.	Governour.
Mr Bernard Toope.	Mr Robert Coker.
Bailiffs.	Assistants.
Mr John Parkins 5.	Edward Dashwood.
Mr Richard Savidge 2.	John Dashwood.
Constables.	Thomas Hiat.
Mr William Paty.	Christopher Way.
Mr William loder.	Sheriff Dorsett.
Mr Lawrence Righton.	Sir Thomas Trenchard.
	Undersheriffe.
	Mr Andrew Keilway.

13 October
This day I rode towards london with Mr Onecipherus Bond,
Roger Cole, and my brother Sam Whiteway. We took Oxford in
our way, and viewed all the Colleges, as also Windsore Castle and
Eaton Colledge, and from thence went to Hampton Court, where
wee saw the King and Queene dine. At lambeth wee saw the
rarityes of Tredescant. And in Morefields I saw a woman delivered
of a child. I returned home 31 October.

20 October
This day My lord Paulet came to Stinsford, with Mr Rolles, Sir John
Stowell, and Sir Ralph Hopton, and lay there a whole moneth
hunting the hare.

22 October
I heard Allison a Coachman and Robins an Alderman of Yarmouth censured in the Star chamber, for slandering the present

Achbishop of yorke Dr Neile, as that in the Kings returne from
Scotland last yeare he should have petitioned him for a toleration
of Popery. The Alderman was fined 500 to the King, £1000 to the
ArchBishop and to acknowledge his fault. Allison was fined £1000
to the King, 500 to the Archbishop and to be whipt in the Pillory at
Yorke, Yarmouth, and Ipswich, where he reported it. Dr Lawde
Archbishop of Canterbury, spake wittily and bitterly and Sir
Thomas Richardson full of girds.

23 October
I heard Bouker the Almanach maker censured by the high commission at Lambeth for fortelling in his Almanach, stirs about Relligion, and dissention between the great men and the Commons.
He was fined [£]40 to be Imprisoned and never more to make any
Almanachs. Dr Boule Bishop of Rochester asked him whether he
forsaw not by his art his fine and censure, to which he answered, no.

24 October
The Lord Mohun put in an informacion to the Star chamber
against Sir James Bag for deceiving the King of £50000 in vittailing
the fleets that went to Rochell and the Isle of Ree.
   My sister Grace Parkins and An Modiford came hither 7 dicto to
have her Jointer sealed, which was done, and they returned 3 daies
after. God took to his mercy my little daughter Elenor Whiteway,
aged about 13 moneths 28 October. She was weaned the 6 of the
said moneth.

6 November
John Guppy had a daughter borne, which had 7 toes upon one
foote.

7 November
This day Heidelberg was taken the 2 time by assault by the Imperialists, under Generall Gallas for the Emperour, and John de
Weerd for the Duke of Bavaria. They could not take the Castell and
so they shortly after left the Towne.

12 November
The Archdeacon Mr fitsharbert visited. Mr Knapton of Chickerell
preached.

14 November
A maid was barbarously ravished and killd neare the lodge at Sherborne: and it was suspected that some of the Earle of Bristols servants were the authors of it, but the matter was smothered.

17 November
This day Sir Thomas Trenchard and Dr Whetcome sate here about a second collection for the repairing for Paules. Every man gave what he would. I gave 2s 6d. There was given by the whole Towne [entry incomplete]

19 November
Mr Rolles hunting in Bradford ground his horse fell under him and brake his necke, and died instantly, Mr Rolles had but little harme.

23 November
The Ministers of london required of their Parishes the tithes of their houses according to the Statute, which paid, would raise some of their livings to £3000 per annum. The Londoners refusing it, they each referred their difference to the King, who was informed of the same.

Joseph Underwood became nonsolvent whereupon some of his creditors gott out an extent upon his goods, executed 19 December.

28 November
This day Mr Thomas Giear, John Blachford, and Thomas Waltham, after a long and chargeable sute followed against them in the Exchequer by Mr John Gardner in the Kings name and his owne, were censured by the Barons upon the Statute of Labourers for werking on undue times, shipping goods at unlawfull howers, and in undue maner: and Mr Thomas Giar who was then Maior, for permitting such unlawfull practises to be done in his house. Mr Giar was fined [£]3000, Mr Blachford 2000 and Mr Thomas Waltham £2000 and all to be imprisoned: but they provided for their liberty. Mr James Gould and Mr John Seward, who went upon the same information, were cleared and discharged by the Court.

About the end of this Terme, the King sent out his writt for the providing of 20 great ships to be made ready by severall citties and port Townes against the 1 March next, to meet at Portesmouth to guard and secure the narrow Seas, and to vindicate the lordship thereof unto the King: London was to furnish 7, the charge whereof amounts to £30000. Dorsett, viz. Poole, Waymouth, Lyme, Wareham, Bridport, Burton, Purbecke and Portland, with the maritime places between them, were to furnish a ship of 400 Tunnes with 260 men, ordinances and vitailes for 6 moneths. They rated themselves thus Waymouth £240, Lyme 160. Poole 150. Purbecke 973. Bridport 80. Wareham 70. And all the rest to be raised upon the sea coasts that ly between these Ports. The Islanders of Purbeck, when Sir Thomas Trenchard came thither of purpose, told him, they could not pay it. Afterwards Waymouth men made a petition to the Counsell that Dorchester might contribute to the charge, which in all they valued at £3500. The Londoners after 2 refusalls were expressely commanded by the King to raise the money, which they did by taking of every man 6 Subsidies. Bristoll and Exon with their members made many excuses.

Sir John Strangewaies desiring to keepe his Christmas in London, desired leave of the King by the Earles of Dorsett and Holland: but the King refused them, and enjoyned him to return and keepe house in the Countrey.

The whole Somer, and all the winter till the 20 December was so dry, that in many places water failed, and they drove their Cattell 3 or 4 miles to water them. Towards Christmas there fell store of raine. All this yeare wheate was sold between 6 and 7s the bushell.

5 December
Here came a french woman that had no hands, but could write, sow, wash and do many other things with her feet. She had a Commission under the seale of the Master of the Revells not allowed here.

The Tavernes being forbidden to sell meate in london, now obtained leave to doe it, paying £30 a peece fine to the King, and an annuall Rent for it.

13 December
Mr Clifford came to Frampton from Yarlington, which he exchanged unto Mr Banger Vicar of Frampton: being of far better value then this.

1634

John Gailards son died between this and Martinstowne upon the way in an extreme hard frost of cold as it is thought upon 17 December.

About this time Sir ferdinand Gorge Captaine of Plimmouth Castell, was made Governour of the Plantations in New England, and one Mr fearly appointed to be the Archbishop of Canterburyes Surrogate in that Countrey.

Mariages of severall persons.
francis Dashwood maried a french woman at Caen 27 July.
Thomas Foxwell maried a second wife at Waymouth 4 August.
Captain Bainard maried Agnes Roy 17 August.
Mr Hugh Thompson maried 27 August.
Mr John Browne Esquire maried to the Lady Wises Daughter 28 August.
William levet maried his maid 2 September.
Joseph Crocker maried Jane Condit 30 September.
Robert fitsjames maried Mr Henry Megs daughter 3 October.
Nicholas Broking and Alice Clark 28 October.
Matthew Harvey mar[ried] Thomasin Dashwood 4 November.
Anne Girdler widow maried to Thomas Morgan 13 November.
Death of sondry persons.
Cousin Alice Gould of Exon 21 July.
John Stevens of Dorchester his wife 4 August.
Mr William Noy, Kings Atturney 10 August.
Mr Tilly Parson of Broadwinsor 18 August.
Cousin Robert Midelton of Limbrick 3 September.
Mr Thomas Gerard of Trent 10 October.
My daughter Elenor Whiteway 28 October.
Mr John Henry Fisher at Wormbs 8 November.
Mr Aldworth Alderman of Bristol 9 November.
Mr Richard Rives of Shaston 23 November.
Cousin Robert Haidon of Caddy 26 November.
Old Mrs Catherine White of Waymouth 1 December.
Mrs Elisabeth Savidge of Blaxworth 15 december.
John Gailard upon the way 17 December.
Sir Thomas Sadleir of Sarum 25 December.

1 January 1634/5
The King pressed the contribution towards the shipping, in all places, yet upon petition he reduced the £3500 that the ports of dorset were to pay, to 2204. And afterwards upon the petition of the Purbeckers presented by Mr Giles Greene, and sollicited by Sir John Bankes the Kings Atturney, Dorchester was ordered to ease Purbecke, whose rate being £550. Dorchester was rated at £200 by Sir Thomas Trenchard Sheriffe who confessed it to be unreasonable, but that he durst not do otherwise, for feare least Mr Greene should complaine of him. This rate was paid with much grudging. In the country it came to £5 upon every £100 land. In this towne they rated the houses and estates of men. I paid 50s towards it. In London of £30000 there was but £12000 collected. Many refused and were sent to Newgate, but were released againe shortly after. In all other places the rate was currently paid, and the fleete provided towards the Spring, which made the French and Hollanders so jealous that they entred into a nearer confederation with one another.

8 January
The Exeter cariers changed their daies of coming hither from Mondays and Wensdayes to Tuesdayes and Thursdayes.

The 9 of this moneth Mr White began to expound the Scriptures in Trinity Church every friday at 10 a clocke.

14 January
At Blandford sessions Sir francis fulford and Sir Walter Earle fell out at the bench about Anthony Barnes, who being suspected of a robbery, the busyness was smothered as much as might be by Sir francis fulford, and Mr Brewen Williams. And Sir Walter Earle was the only man that prosecuted it, so far that some suspicion lighted upon Mr Drew son in law to Sir francis fulford.

This yeare we had an extreme hard winter, with much frost, snow, haile, cold, raine. So that the Thames was frosen and men

went and rode over it 22 January. The inke did freeze in my pen
while I did write. Countrymen could not labour, and therefore
1 february there was an extraordinary Collection in this towne to
releive the extraordinary necessityes of the poore. Many drownd
in snow.

26 January
The Parlement of Dublin prorogued to this time, sate againe this
day.

5 February
Henry Maber was chosen Town Steward in the Roome of Mr
Richard Bury.

12 February
Daniel Toop was born. And the 23 Elisabeth Paty my Goddaughter
was borne.

17 February
Mr Nathaniel Coke was presented to the Parsonage of wotton
neare Lyme by Mr Man of London, and had a very litigious sute
about it against Mr Richard Hide, who claimed right unto it. Their
title was by the Bishop referred to a Jury halfe Clergy men and
halfe Lay. But Mr Cooke obtained it at last.

About this time my unkle John Mounsell settled himselfe to live
at Cardiffe in Wales, having taken home with him Peter Mounsell
who had been here 4 years 4 months.

16 February
This day with running up at a steepe place of Pombery,[16] I fell into
a shortness of breath, with extreme soreness of the brest, for which
I was twice purged by Mr Losse: and had 17 and 8 stooles. And the
18 March I sweated 5 houres. Afterwards the shortness of breath
continuing, I tooke physicke of Mr Olevian, who prescribed in
Althea, tosts in oile, saffron, [?Troves], Powders, drinkes,
Diapheri[tic] and many other things.

25 February
The Citty of London was fined in the Star chamber at £70000 for
suffring of Papists to plant in their plantation of Londonderry in

Ireland, and their patent for that and some other abuses, which they excized, was taken from them, which they much complained off, as having hard measure offred them.

26 dicto. The francis of waymouth was arrested by the Governour of [Honfleur] with all the wooll cloth in her, and was discharged upon payment of 400 [?pistols] to the Governour. Which was raised on the whole lading valued at £3000. His pretence was because there were prohibited marchandise in her, as mixt cloth and Serges. In Roan the Gards brake up many houses and seised on much English goods.

Mr Rulice procured letters patents from the king for a collection over all England for the inhabitants of the Palatinat, who suffred far more under the Swedes and French who came to helpe them, then ever they did under the Spaniards and Imperialists, so that they longed for their Goverment againe. The french lost Udenheim lately, being the strongest fort in those parts. They tooke Spier and the Imperialists tooke Triern, and all the country about the Mosell.

3 March
There were 50 mariners prest at Waymouth to serve the King in the fleete that was providing, who were to draw to Portsmouth, there to be shipt. The like presse there was at all other ports, and those that came not thither on the day limited them, were executed by Martiall Law.

5 March
This day the Assises were held here by Sir John finch, Lord Ch[ief] Justice of Common Pleas and Sir John Denham. Mr Leiford preached. Sir J. finch sate upon the Gaile, he condemned Anthony Barnes for robbery, and John Barfoote for Burglary, and after repreived them both. None were executed. Finch was exceeding high and quicke with the Justices, Lawyers and Bailiffs and all others. The Towne made a new chaire for Mr Sheriff at the Towne Hall.

The newes came that the Hollanders had taken Paraiba from the Portug[uese] in Brasill, whereat they made great triumphes.

At this time Lord Horace Vere shewed the King a petition of a poore tradesman of London, wherein he desired the booke for liberty on the Lords day might be called in, as pernicious to them, and their servants; and laid the blame of it on the Archbishop of Canterbury Laud, who he said, if he had power, would prove more bloudy then Boner, and Nero. The King said, he was an honest man, but wanted discretion.

22 March
The Marquis of fontanelles came extraordinary Ambassadour out of france, and had audience with the King this day. His demand was 1. that our King should enter into a Streiter league with his Maister and the Hollanders against the house of Austria. 2. To have our Queenes dowry confirmed by Act of Parlement according to promise. 3. To have the King pay the money which he promised to contribute towards the wars which the french King makes in Germany. He had but cold entertainment, few of the Nobility went to visit him.

[*The diarist died on* 21 *June* 1635, *a few weeks after this last entry.*]

REFERENCES

1 Entries of household accounts, sundry lists and an inventory of plate, which appear on the fly-leaf and on some of the opening and closing pages of the diary, have been printed together in Appendix 1.
2 This comet came to be regarded as a portent of the Thirty Years War.
3 Sir Walter Ralegh was executed on 29 October 1618.
4 The diarist was married to Elinor Parkins on 14 June 1620.
5 Ferdinand was duke of Gratz before becoming king of Bohemia and Holy Roman Emperor.
6 To make up the number of fifteen capital burgesses. The diarist refers to them as aldermen, though there was legally no such office until 1629. See page 169.
7 Not a hospital in the modern sense but a combination of workhouse, orphanage and craft training school.

8   This was the second great fire in Dorchester within ten years. The first, on 6 August 1613, had burnt 170 houses and caused damage estimated at £39,384.

9   The business referred to is the Dorchester Company, the nucleus of the greater enterprise which founded the colony of Massachusetts.

10 *i.e.* The diarist and his wife set up house on their own for the first time, in the house he had leased from Thomas Brown in the previous May.

11 For the new charter see Appendix 3.

12 See the note for 28 December 1631 on Clara Triandra.

13 It seems likely that this refers to his wife's step-mother Rachel, who, as Rachel Chappell, took John Parkins on 15 April 1621 as her third husband. Rachel is almost an anagram of Clare, 'Triandra' refers to the three husbands, and the diarist's commonplace book gives 1593 as the year of her birth. The entry for 12 July 1631 may refer to the same woman.

14 The diarist's commonplace book contains several pages of 'Directions for limning and instructions in painting by Maister Charles Gage, painter'.

15 Probably the famous Thomas Fuller, who is believed to have been rector of Broadwindsor, Dorset, in 1634.

16 Poundbury, an iron age hill-fort half a mile north-west of Dorchester.

APPENDIX 1

MISCELLANEOUS MATERIAL

1. *On the fly leaf and preliminary pages of the book*

[A coat of arms]

June 9 1627

paid my wife	– 5 –
more 16 June	– 8 –
more 30th dicto	– 7 –
more 6th July	–10–
more 4th August	– 5 –
more 30 August	– 5 –
more 8 September	– 4 –
	2 – 10

Purchased of T. Rodd
28 March 1840

Annus	Pondus	Annus	Pondus	Annus	Pondus
1618		1624		1630	192
1619		1625		1631	196
1620		1626		1632	199
1621		1627		1633	200
1622		1628		1634	
1623		1629		1635	

H.B.D.

	s	
Chaine		8
Mony	1	
Buillion		6
Chaine Mony		
Buillion		

C.N.G.D.

Mony – H Heard	o	o	o

[161]

```
                              J.L.B.D.
    paid 8th Aprill 1626          10s  6d
    more the 12th April           10   0
    more 13th dicto                3   3
    more 21 dicto                 10


                              H.B.C.
    Antico—M———                    1   –   –
    Mony—Nuovo———                  2   –   –
                           pagado    todos
                           [? sestos] Cue
                           Counterchanged


                              C.N.G.C.,ed
    Paper—etc                    4   8
                        Mais il cognoissois [?Lyn]
                              pensero


                     pensen          penseis

                              J.L.B.C.
    M–                             1   10
    [?] V.M.D.                     2   –   –
```

2.   *After the first two paragraphs on page 23*
[*The entries on the following ten lines have been crossed through.*]

27 November
for Henry Browne to speake
to wm brag for £5
to Thomas whetcombe for 16s
to Mr Couth [?qr]
to wm Long 27[s]
to George Smith   £4 18s

28 November
Received of Irwin Church   20
Received of George Glover   10
Receivd off John Parys   10
Received of George Moore   10

                    [162]

1 January 1625/6
paid my wife	3	6
paid the 4th february	12	
paid the 7th dicto for a cap	6	
paid the 15th dicto	5	
paid 18th dicto	5	
paid 21th dicto	5	
paid 4th March	6	
paid 28th 1626	6	
paid a Bodkin	1	6
	02 10	

[*The entries on the following twenty four lines have been crossed through.*]

alla donna mia

paid 9th Aprill 1625	00	10	
more the 27th dicto	01	—	
May the 6th May	00	2	6
June 9th	00	5	
more 11s and 5s	00	5	
b.b.	00	5	
	02	10	

24 June 1625
paid my wife	11
more the 1 July	5
more the 10th	5
more 30th	5
more the 17 August	5
more 23 dicto	6
more 12th September	3
more 22th dicto	5
more 12th October	5
	02 10
more the 22th October	4
more 25th dicto	5
more 5th November	5
more 10th dicto	10
more 21th dicto	11
more 26th dicto	5
more 10th December	5
more in full 31th	5
	02 10

The Inventory of my plate, taken the 10th January 1625.
Two [*deleted*] large beere boules   fower.
A [*deleted*] Silver Tankards two.
A broad wine boule of the old making.
a wine bowle 8 square guilt. [*line deleted*]
Two other guilt bowles [sug....n]. [*line deleted*]
3 wine bowles plaine.
a double Piramides salt.
a Silver Standish etc. [*line deleted*]
Two silver porredge dishes.
6 Silver sawcers. [*line deleted*]
6 Spoones white of one sort.
6 Spoones of severall sorts.
4 Spoones guilt.

John Whiteway Junior. [*line deleted*]
Two bowles plaine. [*line deleted*]
a Trencher salt.

Margaret whiteway. [*line deleted*]
a wine bowle. [*line deleted*]
Two guilt spoones.
a white spoone.
A suger box.

1625 died of the plague in London.

Month	Day	Deaths	Month	Day	Deaths	Month	Day	Deaths
April	7	3	August	4	4550	December	1	015
	14	11		11	4800		08	015
	21	12		18	5205		15	006
	28	23		25	4841		22	001
May	5	30	September	1	3897		29	008
	12	45		8	3157	January	05	008
	19	71		15	2147		12	004
	26	78		22	1994		19	006
JUNE	2	69		29	1236		26	003
	9	91	October	6	538	February	02	004
	16	165		13	511		09	010
	23	239		20	331		16	010
	30	390		27	134		23	008
July	7	590	November	03	089	March	02	001
	14	1744		10	092		09	000
	21	2850		17	048			
10001	28	3590		24	027			

Mr John Parkins owed me at my marriage for my wives porcion £500 which was in September 1620.

He paid me about September 1621

in part of it	200
and then about the Spring Anno 1622	100
more in August 1622	050
more 23th October 1622	050
	400
Rhd 5th November 1622	050
Rhd 13th November 1622	050
Rhd 6th December 1622	030
Rhd 9th January 1622	030
	560
Rhd in full the 10th December 1623	44−06
	604−06

APPENDIX 2

WILL OF WILLIAM WHITEWAY

In the name of God Amen. The first daie of Junne Anno Domini 1635 and
in the yeares of the Raigne of our soveraigne Lord Charles by the grace of
god of England Scotland Fraunce, and Ireland Kinge defendor of the
faith etc. the Eleaventh.

   I William: Whiteway the younger of Dorchester in the Countie of Dorset
Merchaunt being in perfect sence and memory (thankes bee given to
Allmightie god) considering the frailtie of my weake bodie subiect unto
death every moment and yet uncertayne of the tyme when it shall please
god to call me out of this fraile estate, And being desirous to settle in peace
that small porcion which Allmightie god hath bestowed upon me in this
present world Revokeing all former Willes doe make and ordeyne this my
last will and Testament in manner and forme followeing. And First and
principallie I Commend my soule unto the mercy of Allmightie god my
heavenly Father who hath redeemed the same by the onlie merittes death
and passion of his onlie sonne my Lord and Saviour Jesus Christ my bodie
I Comitt to christian buriall To be buried in St Peeters Churche yarde in
Dorchester aforesaide before the porch going into the church. Item I give
and bequeath unto the poore people of the three parishes in Dorchester
aforesaid the summe of Tenn poundes to be equallie distributed between
them at or shortlie after my buriall according to the discrecion of myne
executor herein nominated. Item I give and bequeath unto the free
Schoole of the Towne of Dorchestrer the somme of Twenty poundes to
bee ymployed and be att the disposeing of the Maior, Aldermen, and
Capitall Burgesses of the Burrough of Dorchester or the maior part of
them for the maintenaunce and benefitt of the same Schoole. Item
whereas my Father William Whiteway thelder doth by obligacion stand
bound unto my loving Father in law John Parkins Marchaunt in the some
of One thowsand poundes with Condicion to this or the like effect following that I should leave unto my deere and lovinge wife Elianer the somme
of eight hundred poundes to be paied her within one yeare after my decease Now in dischardge of the said bond and satisfaccion thereof I doe
hereby give and bequeath unto my said wife the somme of Eight hundred
poundes to be paied unto her within one yeare after my decease. Allso I
give unto my said wife the one halfe of all my plate and somuch of
ymplementes of howseholdstuffe as shalbe worth thirty poundes and that

[166]

my said wife shall choose the same out of all my ymplementes of howse. Item I give and bequeath unto that child which my loveing wife now goeth withall the some of three hundred poundes to bee paied unto him if hee bee a sonne att the age of one and twenty yeares and if itt be a daughter at the age of eighteene yeares or att her daye of marriage which of them shall first happen and in the meane tyme the profittes thereof shall goe towardes the breedeing upp and maintenaunce of the same childe. But if itt shall happen that the same childe shall dye before the said legacy shall bee payeable* then I give unto my loving brothers Samuell Whitewaye, and John Whitewaye, and to my loving sister Mary Whiteway the somme of six poundes thirteene shillinges and fower pence apeece to bee bestowed in a peece of plate for every of them within one yeare after my decease in remembraunce of my love towardes them. Item I give unto Mr John White preacher of gods holye worde of Dorchester Forty shillinges to be bestowed in a Ringe for him. Item I give into my lovinge sister in lawe Mistress Elizabeth Bull one gold ringe of the price of forty shillinges in token of my love to her. Item I give unto my maide servaunt Luce Hickson the some of Forty shillinges. Item I give unto my servant Katherine Davis if shee live with me untill my death the some of Ten shillinges. All the Residue of my goods whatsoever moveable and unmoveable not before given and bequeathed my debts and legacies being paied and my funerall expences and all other charges paied and discharged out of mine estate, I give and bequeath unto my deere and lovinge father William Whiteway thelder whome I make and ordeyne executor in trust of this my last will and Testament, to and for the use and benefitt of my lovinge sonne William Whiteway whose education I doe comitt to my said Father desireing him for godes glory and my childes good out of my said estate to breed him upp and to bestowe and lay out in purchase all or some parte of the said estate hereby appointed to my sonne William in lande, leases Annuyties or otherwise as to my said executor shall seeme to bee most beneficiall for my said sonne. And my Will and meaneing is, and I doe hereby declare my Will to bee, that my said executor shall bee from tyme to tyme freed and discharged of all chardges and disbursementes whatsoever in the collectinge, getting in, sueing or procureing in and orderinge of myne estate out of my personall estate which I shall leave at my decease. And I doe hereby appointe and ordeyne Mr John Parkins my Father in lawe, and my Cosen Mr Dennis Bonde to be my Overseers of this my last will and Testament desireing them to see the same affected in all pointes and I give to each of them a Ringe twenty shillinges price apeece in remembraunce of my love to them. In Witness whereof I have hereunto sett my hand and seale the day and yeare first above written

W. Whiteway

Signed sealed and acknowledged to be the last will of the within named
William Whitewaye in the presence of us
Jo Perkins and [mark of] Gilbert Loder,
Marke of John Allambrigg, Andrew Middleton

Proved at London 7 September 1635

(*PRO, Prerogative Court of Canterbury*, 94 *Sadler* 1635)

*[*There appears to be a lacuna in this section of the will.*]

APPENDIX 3

THE CHARTERS OF 1610 and 1629

Dorchester gained its status as a borough in Saxon times, acquiring various
liberties and privileges by custom during succeeding centuries. These ancient rights were formalized and the borough was incorporated by the
charter which the town obtained from James I in 1610.

Under this charter all effective authority was vested in fifteen "Capital
Burgesses" (the "Fifteen"), who held office for life and were empowered
to make up any vacancies in their number by co-option. Each year at
Michaelmas two bailiffs were elected by and from the Fifteen, to act as
chief officers of the borough for the next twelve months. These two
bailiffs, together with their predecessors in office and with the recorder
(law officer) of the corporation, served as justices of the peace; they had
jurisdiction over all but the most serious crimes committed within the
borough boundaries, magistrates from elsewhere in the county being forbidden to meddle in the town's affairs. The burgesses were also given
power to make ordinances (by-laws) for the better government of the
town, provided these were not repugnant to the laws of the realm. The au-
thorities were thus able to exercise strict control over every aspect of the
townspeople's social and economic life.

In 1629 a new charter was secured, which gained yet more privileges. There were still fifteen capital burgesses, but a mayor now took precedence over the two bailiffs, six of the senior capital burgesses were now dignified with the title of alderman, and a second municipal council was established. This was the "Common Council of the Free Men of the Borough", which in effect confirmed by royal patent the Company of Freemen, a body which had been set up by ordinance in 1621. It was composed of twenty-four craftsmen, one of whose number was to be chosen as "Governor", while five others were to act as his assistants. Since the Fifteen appointed all the members of the council and since its officers held their positions only at the pleasure of the Fifteen, this was not the liberalizing measure it might appear but exactly the opposite. A year later, in 1630, the freemen of the borough were organized into five companies, each with its own warden, of merchants, clothiers, ironmongers, fishmongers and leatherworkers, and in these groups were included artisans of sixty-eight different crafts. Minute regulations governed commerce and industry within the walls, and alien craftsmen were banned from the town. It was a highly authoritarian regime.

The merchant-gentlemen who obtained the charters of 1610 and 1629 – the Blachfords, Goulds, Parkins, Whiteways, and so on – took care to have themselves named in the patent of incorporation as the first capital burgesses. In this way they established themselves legally as a powerful, self-perpetuating oligarchy ready to guide the destiny of Dorchester. Their unofficial leader was John White, the Calvinist rector of Holy Trinity, whose stern zeal made the town a model of Puritan autocracy.

APPENDIX 4

THE WHITEWAY FAMILY TREE

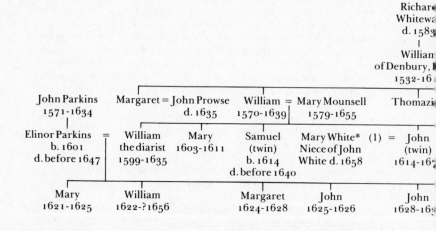

Richard
Whitewa
d. 1583

William
of Denbury, I
1532-16

John Parkins 1571-1634	Margaret = John Prowse d. 1635	William = Mary Mounsell 1570-1639 │ 1579-1655	Thomazi
Elinor Parkins b. 1601 d. before 1647 =	William the diarist 1599-1635	Mary 1603-1611	Samuel (twin) b. 1614 d. before 1640	Mary White* Niece of John White d. 1658 (1) =	John (twin) 1614-16?
Mary 1621-1625	William 1622-?1656		Margaret 1624-1628	John 1625-1626	John 1628-169

NOTE

Most of these dates have been taken from a list in the diarist's commonplace book and must therefore be Old Style. A transcript of the list has been published in "The Commonplace Book of a Dorsetshire Man (A.D. 1625-1635)", by the Revd. W. Miles Barnes, in *Proceedings of the Dorset Natural History and Antiquarian Field Club*, XVI (1895), 59-74. The dates of William's youngest brother and of his children, taken from his diary, are given New Style.

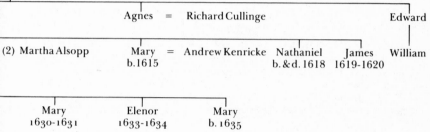

= Thomasin Gould
of Staverton
d. 1613

Agnes = Richard Cullinge   Edward

(2) Martha Alsopp   Mary = Andrew Kenricke   Nathaniel   James   William
                b. 1615   b. & d. 1618   1619-1620

Mary   Elenor   Mary
1630-1631   1633-1634   b. 1635

* According to a pedigree preserved in the *Hampshire Visitation* of 1634 John's first wife Mary was daughter of Stephen White, of Stanton St John, Oxon., and niece of John White, Rector of Holy Trinity, Dorchester; *v. Publications of the Harleian Society*, 64 (1913). Six surviving children of this marriage were named in John Whiteway's will.

APPENDIX 5

BIOGRAPHICAL NOTES

These cover many of the Dorset people mentioned in the diary and are chiefly based on notes compiled by Thomas D. Murphy.

ADYN, JOHN (d. 1632). Brewer of Dorchester. Fire of 1623 started on his property in Trinity parish. A bailiff and burgess of 1582-83 had the same name.

ASHLEY, SIR ANTHONY (1551-1628). Member of important family situated at Wimborne St Giles and brother of Sir Francis Ashley. Courtier to Queen Elizabeth and Clerk of the Privy Council. Knighted for services on Cadiz expedition in 1596. Spent his later years engaged in experiments in farming and was a benefactor of his village. His daughter, Anne, married Sir John Cooper, Bt., and was mother of Anthony Ashley Cooper, first Earl of Shaftesbury.

ASHLEY, SIR FRANCIS (1569-1635). Younger brother of Sir Anthony. Successful lawyer. MP for Dorchester in 1614, 1621 and 1625. Expressly named Recorder for life in the new borough charter of 1629, which was probably secured with his aid. Active in London and Dorchester until his sudden death in 1635. His Dorchester house was the old Friary. His daughter, Dorothy, married Denzil Holles.

BALL, JOHN (d. 1640). Rector of Langton Matravers from 1618. Related to the diarist and to John White. Rector of All Saints, Dorchester, for a few months 1628-29.

BARKER, RICHARD (d. 1621). Shoemaker of Dorchester. Burgess in 1593. Capital burgess at death.

BATEMAN, RICHARD (b. 1599). Merchant of London. Son of Robert Bateman. Connected in French trade with James Gould of Dorchester.

BATEMAN, ROBERT (b. 1565). Merchant of London, trading with France. Benefactor of Dorchester. Married Joan Mounsell, the diarist's aunt, in 1594. Jane and Susan, "cousins" of the diarist, were probably his daughters.

BENN, WILLIAM (1600-81). Born in Cumberland. Chaplain to the Marchioness of Northampton. Invited by John White to Dorchester. Rector of All Saints from 1629 to 1662. More extreme than John White, and considered by many as largely responsible for Dorchester's reputation as a hot-bed of Puritan sedition. Deprived in 1662 for non-conformity. Licensed as a non-conforming teacher in 1672.

BLACHFORD, JOHN. Wool merchant of Dorchester. Governor of company of freemen 1622-23. Capital burgess 1623. Bailiff 1626-27 and 1632-33. Trading contacts with Spain, Virginia and Newfoundland. Interested in colonizing projects in New England. Lived in France, perhaps to evade smuggling charges, from about 1633 to 1639, when he was superseded as capital burgess because of continued absence. Probably brother to Richard and Thomas (below).

BLACHFORD, RICHARD (d. 1652). Clothier of Dorchester. Burgess 1610. Bailiff 1621-22, 1627-28. Assistant to the governor of freemen 1629-30. Mayor 1630-31, 1647-48. Had a daughter, Edith. It was probably his son, Richard, who was admitted freeman as merchant 1624.

BLACHFORD, THOMAS. Merchant of Dorchester. On council of freemen 1629-30. Took wife and her sister to France 1632. In difficulties with king's customs collector 1634. Living in France 1644.

BOND, DENNIS (1588-1658). Woollen-draper of Dorchester. Close friend of John White. Bailiff 1623, 1630-31. Mayor 1635. MP 1640. Named as a Commissioner to try the King 1648. Member of Council of State 1649-53; president thereof 1652-53. MP for Weymouth and Melcombe Regis 1654 and 1656. Related to diarist through mother, Margaret (née Pitt), and through first wife, Joan Gould. Godfather to his daughter Elenor 1633. Appointed overseer of the diarist's will. Also witnessed the will of William Whiteway, senior.

BOND, JOHN (1555-1633). Of Lutton in the Isle of Purbeck. Married Margaret, daughter of Richard Pitt of Weymouth, 1583. Mayor of Weymouth 1585, 1599, 1612. Father of Dennis.

BOND, ONESIPHERUS (1612-1635). Merchant. Brother of Dennis, who moved burgesses of Dorchester that he be admitted freeman 1633.

BRADISH, DR. (d. 1638). Rector of Puddletown and Athelhampton from 1611. Investor in the Dorchester Company. A leader in opposition to the Fifteen, September 1631.

BROWNE, SIR JOHN (c. 1588-1627). Son of John Browne, Esquire of Frampton, Married Jane, daughter of Sir Henry Portman of Orchard, Somerset. Sheriff 1588, 1616, 1618. Deputy-Lieutenant 1625-26. John (below) and George (1583-1631), a lawyer, were his sons.

BROWNE, JOHN (1581-1659). Son of Sir John, of Frampton. Married Eliza, daughter of Sir George Trenchard, of Wolfeton, 1607, and had two sons, John (d. 1670) and George. MP for Bridport 1614, 1620, 1625. Sheriff of Dorset 1616, 1618, 1633-34. MP for Dorset 1641. Close friend of John White and William Benn. Investor in the Dorchester Company and other schemes of colonization.

BULL, GEORGE. Probably Dr George Bull of Wells, who later became Bishop of St David's. In 1631 presented religious works to the Dorchester library. Married

Elizabeth Parkins, the diairist's sister-in-law 1625. He was godfather to the diarist's daughter Mary 1630; his wife was godmother to John the first 1625.

BURY, RICHARD (d. 1662). Grocer of Dorchester. Constable 1626-27, 1629-30. Governor of freemen 1628-29. Assistant to governor 1629-30, 1632-33. Burgess 1633. Bailiff 1633-34, 1647. Mayor 1640, 1651. Investor in the Dorchester Company.

BUSHRODE, JOHN. Clothier of Dorchester. Probably son of Richard (below). Freeman 1626. Constable 1631-32, 1632-33. Assistant to governor 1629-30, 1633-34. Burgess 1639. Bailiff 1651. Mayor 1655-56. Steward of the hospital 1651-56.

BUSHRODE, RICHARD (d. 1628). Haberdasher and merchant-adventurer of Dorchester. Bailiff 1621-22, 1626-27. MP for Dorchester 1626. Investor in Dorchester Company and subsequent ventures. Thomas, a merchant, probably his son, married Wilmot Parkins, sister-in-law of the diarist 1629.

BUTLER, MATTHEW. Shoemaker of Dorchester. Assistant to governor of freemen 1623-25, 1629-31. Constable 1627-28.

CHAFFIN, BAMPFIELD (d. 1644). Esquire of Folke. MP for Bridport 1628. Sheriff 1625. Besieged and captured by parliamentary forces. Died at Exeter and buried in the cathedral 1644.

CHAPPELL, RACHEL. Widow of Richard (d. 9 Feb. 1621), son of Elinor Chappell of Exeter (d. 1611). On 15 April 1621 Rachel married John Parkins, father-in-law of the diarist, as her third husband. Elinor Chappell was thus step-grandmother of Elenor, the diarist's wife. (See also note 13 on page 120.)

CHEEKE, ROBERT (c. 1572-1627). Master of the free school from his arrival in Dorchester 1595. Rector of All Saints from 1617. Benefactor of the town, and highly respected. The diarist was one of his pupils and journeyed with him to Oxford 1614.

CHUBB, MATTHEW (d. 1617). Goldsmith of Dorchester. Bailiff 1593, 1602, 1610. Authorized by the King on 12 Nov. 1613 to advance £1,000 for rebuilding Dorchester after the great fire of 1613, the sum to be deducted from the next subsidy. He rebuilt the George Inn, burned in the fire. With his wife, Margaret, he endowed an almshouse for women.

CHURCHILL, JOHN (c. 1570-1621). Clothier of Stinsford. Son of William Churchill of Dorchester. Member of a wealthy family long associated with Dorchester. Benefactor of the town. Survived by his wife, Elinor, and son, William.

CLARKE, EDWARD (d. 1630). Clerk. Assistant to John White 1620-25, until he moved to Taunton. Baptised diarist's second daughter, Margaret (Margery), 1624.

COKE, JOHN (d. 1641). Mercer and fustian-weaver of Puddletown and Dorchester. First governor of the hospital 1616-34. Governor of freemen 1625-26, 1629-32.

Lieutenant in county militia 1627. A leader in revolt against Fifteen 1631. Twice under-sheriff.

COKER, ROBERT (*c*. 1579-1655). Goldsmith of Ashbosam. Assistant to governor of freemen 1621-22, 1627-28, 1629-30. Governor of freemen 1634-35. Investor in the Dorchester Company. Married Martha, daughter of William Chubb of Frome Selwood. His daughter Joan married a Matthew Chubb.

CONDIT, JOHN (d. 1634). Tailor of Dorchester. Assistant to governor of freemen 1621-22, 1623-24. Sergeant-at-mace 1624; also in 1629, when he was go-between for the burgesses to John Arnold, courtier, who secured the charter from Charles I. Beadle of the company of freemen 1629-30. Sergeant-at-arms 1634.

COOKE, PATROCLUS (d. 1658). Beadle of company of freemen of Dorchester 1621. Sergeant-at-mace 1624 and 1634. One of leaders in revolt against the Fifteen 1631. Burgess 1631.

COOKE, NATHANIEL (d. 1642). Clerk, nephew of John White. Usher at the free school 1632. Rector of Wootton Fitzpaine from 1638.

COOPER, SIR JOHN (d. 1631). Member of an ancient family of Rockbourne, Hampshire. Baronet 1622. MP for Poole 1625, 1628. His first wife was Anne, daughter of Sir Anthony Ashley, who died 1628. Anthony Ashley Cooper, first Earl of Shaftesbury, was their son.

DASHWOOD, EDMOND (1588-1642). Mercer of Dorchester. Friend of John White. Burgess 1620. Constable 1623-25. Bailiff 1625-26, 1631-32, 1633-34. Mayor 1632-33. Contributor to the hospital, investor in the Dorchester Company and other ventures in New England.

DASHWOOD, EDWARD (d. 1667). Clothier of Dorchester. Probably son of Edmond. Assistant to governor of freemen 1629-30, 1634-35. Governor 1633-34. Burgess 1636. Ensign in parliamentary forces of the borough 1643. Mayor 1662-63.

DASHWOOD, FRANCIS. Mercer. Son of Edmond. Admitted to company of freemen 1623, as apprentice to John Blachford. Married a Frenchwoman 1634.

DERBY, HENRY. Mercer, probably brother of William (below). Constable 1624-28. Assistant to governor of freemen 1625-26, 1629-30, 1633-34. Governor 1626-27. Ensign in county militia 1627. Warden of company of merchants 1630. Moved to Beaminster 1634.

DERBY, WILLIAM (*c*. 1588-1649). Mercer of Beaminster and Dorchester. Burgess 1626. Contributed to expenses of 1629 charter, in which he was named bailiff and town clerk, an office he held 1625-48. Bailiff again 1633-39. Under-sheriff of Dorset 1640. Investor in Dorchester Company and other ventures in New England. A daughter married John White's nephew.

DEVENISH, BENJAMIN (1574-1643). Of Bradford Peverell. Proprietor of an alehouse, the Golden Falcon, in 1619. Clerk of Dorchester brewhouse 1623-40. Investor in the Dorchester Company.

DEVENISH, THOMAS (b. *c.* 1599). Upholsterer of Dorchester. Freeman 1621. Sergeant-at-mace 1622, 1626. Keeper of county gaol, but ousted 1628 and 1634-37 because of abuses in this office. Undersheriff 1632-33. Investor in the Dorchester Company.

ERLE, CHRISTOPHER (d. 1612). Esquire of Sturminster Marshall. Brother of Sir Walter Erle. Recorder of Lyme Regis and its MP. His son, also Christopher (c. 1590-1634), was MP for Weymouth 1621, Lyme 1624 and 1628, Poole 1626.

ERLE, SIR WALTER (1586-1665). Member of notable family of Charborough. Knight of the Shire 1626, 1628. Sheriff 1619. MP at various times for Poole, Weymouth and Lyme Regis. Friend of John White. Investor in the Dorchester Company, for which he secured an indenture for colonisation in New England. Governor of the company. Vigorous opponent of Charles I in parliament and in the field, but not successful as a general. Repulsed by Lady Bankes in his assault on Corfe Castle. Military governor of Dorchester 1643, but fled at the approach of the Royalists.

FISHER, JOHN HENRY (d. 1634). Refugee from Palatinate 1626. Returned to Germany 1633.

FITZHERBERT, RICHARD (d. 1653). Vicar of Gussage All Saints 1621. Archdeacon of Dorset 1621.

FITZJAMES, LEWESTON (*c.* 1574-1638). Son and heir of Sir John, of Leweston. Sheriff of Dorset 1627-28.

FREKE, SIR THOMAS (*c.* 1563-1633). Of Iwerne Courtney. Twice Knight of the Shire. Deputy-lieutenant for about thirty years, and a respected figure in the county. Co-owner, with his son, of the ship *Leopard* of Weymouth, largest of the Dorset privateers.

FREKE, JOHN. Son and heir of Sir Thomas. MP for Weymouth 1621, 1624. Married Arundell, daughter of Sir George Trenchard of Wolfeton. Co-owner of the *Leopard*, which was commanded by Nicholas Strangeways, his wife's brother-in-law.

GOLSNEY, WILLIAM. Of Holnest, Dorchester. Undersheriff 1624-25, 1627-28. Investor in the Dorchester Company.

GOULD, CHRISTOPHER (d. 1668). Master of school in Trinity parish from 1633.

GOULD, EDWARD. Eldest son of John Gould of Staverton, Devon. Brother of John Gould of Dorchester (below) and of Thomasin, who was the diarist's grandmother. He had five sons who became men of substance: William (below); Edward, probably the "cousin" who died at Venice 1632; Henry; Nicholas, who made a fortune trading in France; James (below); also a daughter, Alice.

GOULD, GEORGE (d. 1633). Clothier of Dorchester. Governor of hospital 1627.

GOULD, JAMES (1593-1676). Clothier of Dorchester. Second son of John Gould. Godfather of diarist's son in 1628; his wife, Margery, was godmother to his second daughter 1624. Burgess 1623-24. Bailiff 1627-28, 1631-32. Mayor 1633. Royalist in Civil War and removed as burgess. Connected in business with his cousin Nicholas and sometime resident in France. Investor in the Dorchester Company. Benefactor of the town.

GOULD, JAMES (d. 1650). Merchant of Exeter. Son of Edward Gould. Successful in business. Settled in Exeter, where he held several important offices.

GOULD, JOAN (1549-1630). Widow of James Gould of Fordington, probably the "old cousin" who died at Bath in 1613. A wealthy woman, owning property in Dorchester and Fordington. Godmother to diarist's son William 1622, and also to his daughter Mary. Benefactress of Dorchester and neighbouring places; also of John White.

GOULD, JOHN (*c.* 1558-1630). Merchant of Upwey and Dorchester. Brother of Edward and great-uncle of the diarist. Married Joan Benvenue of Abbotsbury. Burgess 1610. Substantial property owner. Benefactor of town. His son, also John (b. 1589), was a merchant too, trading to France.

GOULD, WILLIAM (d. 1635). Merchant of Hayes near Exeter. Son of Edward. Married Alice Taylor and had a daughter Elizabeth. Investor in the Dorchester Company.

GREENE, GILES (d. 1656). Of Afflington in Purbeck and of Motcombe. MP for Weymouth 1621, 1626; and for Corfe Castle 1625, 1628. Investor in the Dorchester Company.

GREY, ANGEL. Esquire of Kingston Maurward. Sheriff 1629. On bad terms with his Puritan neighbours in Dorchester. Royalist during the Civil War, when his farm at Kingston was sequestered.

GYEAR, DAVID (d. 1633). Merchant of Weymouth and Melcombe Regis. Related, perhaps through his wife, to the diarist. Magistrate and sometime mayor of Weymouth. Accused of sharp practice in politics and also in smuggling.

GYEAR, THOMAS. Merchant and magistrate of Weymouth and Melcombe Regis. Related to the diarist. Part owner of a privateer 1626. Heavily fined for conspiring to evade customs dues 1635. Fines not paid by 1651.

HASELBURY, SIMON. Clothier of Dorchester. Another Simon, probably his son, admitted freeman 1621. Assistant to governor of freemen 1624-25, 1627-28. Named on common council of freemen in 1629 Charter.

HAYNE, OLIVER (*c.* 1563-1622). Gentleman of Dorchester. Burgess 1610. His son, Morgan, made freeman 1621. Receiver of the company of freemen 1621.

Investor in the Dorchester Company and other ventures in New England. Moved to Newcastle-on-Tyne. Related to the diarist.

HIATT, THOMAS (d. 1639). Mercer of Dorchester. Freeman 1621. Constable 1630-32. Assistant to governor of freemen 1634-35.

HILL, JOHN (1589-c.1657). Ironmonger of Dorchester. Elected burgess and alderman 1621. First governor of the company of freemen 1621. MP for Dorchester 1628. Bailiff 1631-32. Treasurer of the county 1633. Mayor 1636-37. Investor in the Dorchester Company. Owned several privateers. Benefactor of Dorchester.

HOLLES, DENZIL (1599-1680). Son of John, first Earl of Clare. MP for Dorchester 1628-29. Important figure in parliamentary oppostition to Crown. Imprisoned in Tower 1629. MP for Dorchester 1640, speaking on behalf of Commons. (See *Dictionary of National Biography*).

HOPFF, JOHN CASPAR. Refugee from Palatinate 1627. Married Katherine Gardiner, John White's niece, 1633.

HORSEY, SIR GEORGE (d. 1645). Of Clifton Maybank and Melcombe Horsey. Entirely alienated a great estate. Spent last years in poverty, and died a debtor in prison.

HUMFRY, JOHN (1597-c.1652). Son of Michael (below) of Dorchester. Treasurer of the Dorchester Company. Actively engaged in this and other colonizing ventures. Sailed to New England 1634, but returned 1641. His son, Colonel John Humfry, was sword bearer before judges of Charles I.

HUMFRY, MICHAEL (d. 1626). Esquire of East Chaldon and Dorchester. Alderman of Dorchester 1625. Died while MP for Dorchester. The diarist was elected to sit out his term.

IRONSIDE, GILBERT (1588-1671). Rector of Winterbourne Steepleton from 1619, and of Winterbourne Abbas 1625. One of the leaders in revolt against Fifteen 1631. Royalist in Civil War. Bishop of Bristol 1661. His father, Ralph (d.1628), and brother, also Ralph (d. 1683), were rectors in succession of Long Bredy.

JOLLIFFE, HUMPHREY (c. 1583-1653). Lawyer in Dorchester. Steward of manors of Sir Edward Lawrence 1627-31. Mayor 1633. Investor in the Dorchester Company.

JOLLIFFE, WILLIAM (d. 1660?). Woollen-draper of Dorchester. Bailiff 1623-24, 1629-30. Mayor 1633-34.

KNAPTON, TRISTRAM. Rector of Chickerell from 1633.

KNAPTON, RINALDO. Of Dorchester. Married Cassandra, daughter of Thomas Sparrow, keeper of the county gaol, whom he succeeded in that office. Under-sheriff 1628.

LAWRENCE, SIR EDWARD (1562-1629). Of Creech Grange, Isle of Purbeck. Sheriff of Dorset 1621-22. MP for Wareham 1625.

LAWRENCE, JONATHAN (*c.* 1600-1664). Son of William (below). Assistant to John White 1632-33. Rector of Winterborne Kingston 1641-42; of Haselbury Bryan 1647; of Upwey from 1648.

LAWRENCE, ROBERT. Shoemaker of Dorchester. Constable 1622-23, 1633-34. Warden of company of shoemakers 1630.

LAWRENCE, WILLIAM. Clerk. Second son of Richard of Winterbourne Steepleton and half-brother of George, the heir. Three times married.

LEVETT, WILLIAM. Weaver of Dorchester. Admitted freeman 1622.

LONG, JOHN (d. 1632). Bookseller of Dorchester. Constable 1621-22, 1627-28. Assistant to governor of freeman 1623-24, 1625-26. Governor of freemen 1627-28, 1629-30. Elected capital burgess 1631. Bailiff 1632-33.

LOSSE, FREDERICK. Physician, graduate of Heidelberg. Probably refugee from Palatinate. Friend and physician of John White. Given fee for taking care of "the poore of the Towne" 1650. Capital burgess 1658. Treated diarist shortly before his death 1635.

MABER, HENRY (1588-1667). Clothier of Sydling St Nicholas and Dorchester. Constable 1626-29. Member of council of freemen 1629-30, 1630-31, 1633-34; its receiver 1629-30. Governor of freemen 1632-33. Burgess 1633. Town steward 1635. Bailiff 1648-49. Mayor 1653-54.

MANUELL, HUGH (d. 1634). Blacksmith and freeman of Dorchester.

MARTIN, AMIAS. Mercer of Seaborough, Somerset. Freeman of Dorchester 1623. Member of council of freemen 1626-27, 1629-30.

MARTIN, WILLIAM (d. 1633). Sieve-maker of Dorchester. Freeman 1621.

MEECH, DEBORAH (1603-34). Daughter of William Lawrence. Called "cousin" by diarist.

MELLER, SIR JOHN (d. 1650). Son and heir of Sir Robert (d. 1624), of Little Bredy, and nephew of Giles. Married Mary Swinnerton, daughter of Lord Mayor of London 1611. Captain of Dorset horse 1628. Sheriff of Dorset 1630; of Oxfordshire 1633. MP for Wareham 1628.

MIDDLETON, ROBERT (d. 1624). Merchant of London and probably of Weymouth-Melcombe Regis. Member of chartered company of merchants trading to France 1612. MP for Melcombe Regis 1603-04. Probably married diarist's aunt. Of his children, Elizabeth, John, Robert and Peter, the last seems to have been apprenticed to the Whiteways, before engaging in Turkey trade 1627. Peter was godfather to diarist's second son, John, 1625.

MILLER, WILLIAM. Brewer of Fordington. Company of freemen 1634.

MOHUN, SIR MAXIMILLIAN (1596-1672). Son of Maximillian of Fleete. Royalist in Civil War. Imprisoned at Weymouth. Estate sequestered.

MOHUN, WALTER (d. 1638). Rector of Broadmayne from 1617, Poxwell 1623.

MOUNSELL, MARY (1579-1655). Daughter of John Mounsell and Joan (née Pitt). Married William Whiteway 1598. Mother of diarist. Descended from Peter Mounsell of Launceston, one of whose sons, John, was mayor of Weymouth 1577. Several relatives in Dorchester area. A younger cousin, Peter, student at Dorchester free school 1632, boarded as apprentice with Whiteways until 1635, when he moved with his father to Cardiff.

MUNDIN, GEORGE. Tailor of Dorchester. Council of freemen 1626-27, 1628-32. One of leaders in revolt against Fifteen 1631.

MUNDIN, WILLIAM. Tailor of Dorchester. Freeman 1626.

NAPIER, SIR NATHANIEL (d. 1635). Only son of Sir Robert (below). Sheriff 1620-21. Deputy-lieutenant 1625-26. MP for Dorset 1625-6, Wareham 1626, Milborne Port 1628-9. His eldest son, Sir Gerard (1606-73), pursued an equivocal course during Civil War; later a favourite of Charles II.

NAPIER, SIR ROBERT (d. 1615). Of More Crichel and Middlemarsh, Dorset. Chief Baron of the Exchequer in Ireland. Sheriff of Dorset 1606. He and his wife Lady Magdalen (d. 1625), made notable benefactions to Dorchester, including the borough almshouses, Napper's Mite.

NEWBURGH, WALTER (c. 1596-1631). Rector of Symondsbury 1624-31. Probably son of William, "old Mr Newburgh" (d. 1632).

NICHOLS, FERDINANDO. Fellow student at New College, Oxford, with John White, whom he assisted at St Peter's, Dorchester, 1625-27. A "grand presbyterian, if not worse". Later moved to Sherborne.

NICHOLS, MATTHIAS (c. 1586-1631). Elder brother of Ferdinando. Rector of Mells 1619, Plymouth 1630. A noted Puritan. Associated with John White in schemes for colonizing New England. Member of Dorchester and New England Companies. Widow moved to Dorchester 1634.

NICHOLLS, PHILIP (d. 1632). Tailor of Dorchester. Freeman 1621. Accused of criticising John White 1630.

OLEVIAN, FRANCIS ANTHONY (d. 1642). Physician and astrologer. Religious refugee from Germany. Treated diarist shortly before his death.

PARKINS, JOHN (1571-1640). Merchant of Dorchester. Father-in-law of diarist. Burgess and bailiff by 1610. MP 1621. Bailiff for fifth time 1634-35. Influential magistrate. Benefactor of Dorchester. By his first wife, Wilmot (1583-1617), he had eight children, all of whom predeceased him, except the eldest: Elinor (b. 1601), wife of diarist; Margaret (1602-27); William (1604-31), merchant of Dorchester and Wareham; Wilmot (d. 1633); John (1607-27), who died in Florence; Eliza (1608-35); Joseph (d. 1633); Martha (d. 1627). By his second marriage, to Rachel Chappell of Exeter, already twice widowed, he had a daughter Mary (1625-45), and a son John (b. 1629).

PATY, JOSEPH. Clothier of Dorchester. Assistant to governor of freemen 1621-22, 1625-26, 1629-30, 1632-33. Governor of freemen 1623-24, 1631-32. Warden of company of clothiers 1630-31. A leader of revolt against the Fifteen 1631. Captain of borough militia 1643. Called "uncle" by diarist. Both he and his wife were godparents to children of the diarist.

PATY, WILLIAM (b. 1606). Clothier of Dorchester. Admitted freeman 1630. Constable 1634-35. Burgess 1652. Diarist was godfather to one of his daughters.

PELE, EDWARD (*c*. 1582-1643). Vicar of Fordington 1617-28. Rector of Compton Valence 1628. With John White, represented Dorset at Assembly of Divines 1643.

PELHAM, THOMAS. Of Compton Valence, Dorset. Captain in Dorset militia 1622-29.

PHILIPS, HUGH. Grocer of Dorchester. Freeman 1623.

PITT, EDWARD. Eldest son of Sir William Pitt of Stepleton, Dorset. Burgess of Poole and MP for Poole 1626.

PITT, JOHN (*c*. 1547-1627). Merchant and shipowner of Lanehouse, Bridport and Weymouth. Mayor of Weymouth 1618 and MP for Poole 1623. Investor in Newfoundland fishing trade and in Dorchester Company. Brother to diarist's maternal grandmother. Married Agnes Davidge. Children included Joseph, Alice (d. 1626) and Phineas.

PITT, MATTHEW (d. 1624). Merchant of Weymouth. MP 1621 and 1624. Described by diarist as "cousin".

READE, THOMAS (d. 1634). Alehouse keeper of Dorchester. Freeman 1622.

REEVE, GABRIEL (b. 1593). Master of the free school at Dorchester 1627-50.

RIGHTON, LAWRENCE. Cutler of Dorchester. Freeman 1621. Constable 1634-35. Governor of freemen 1651. Burgess 1658.

RULIZIUS, JOHN NICHOLAS. Refugee minister from Palatinate. Probably arrived in Dorchester 1626. Assistant to John White 1628-31. Agent for Queen of Bohemia 1634.

SAVAGE, RICHARD (d. 1669). Woollen-draper of Bloxworth. Assistant to governor of freemen 1624-25, 1627-28. Bailiff 1630-31, 1634-35. Mayor 1639-40, 1651-52. Governor of hospital 1634. Investor in Dorchester Company. Captain in militia for Parliament in Civil War. Brother of William, counsellor-at-law.

SCHLOER, FREDERICK. Refugee minister from Palatinate. Arrived Dorchester 1627. Licensed to preach by Bishop of Bristol 1630.

SIMS, WILLIAM (d. 1633). Blacksmith of Dorchester. Freeman 1631.

[181]

SPARROW, THOMAS (d. 1629). Keeper of county gaol 1628-29.

SPICER, JOHN (d. 1623). MP for Dorchester 1603-11. Burgess 1610.

STRANGWAYS, SIR JOHN (1587-1664). Member of ancient family of Melbury Sampford and Abbotsbury. Married Grace, daughter of Sir George Trenchard. MP for Dorset 1614-15, 1620-21, 1623-24, 1628-9; for Melcombe Regis 1625; for Weymouth 1626, 1640, 1641 and 1663. Influential in county. Though imprisoned for opposing the King's policies in parliament, he was a staunch Royalist in the Civil War, like his son Giles, and both suffered for their loyal stand.

STRODE, SIR JOHN (d. 1642). Of Chantmarle, Dorset. MP for Bridport 1620-21, 1625.

STRODE, SIR RICHARD (1584-1669). Of Chalmington, Dorset, and of Newnham park, Devon. MP at various times for Beer Alston, Bridport and Plympton. On committee of Dorchester Company.

TAYLOR, FERDINAND. Vicar of Fleet from 1629.

TERRY, JOSIAS (1597-1667). Haberdasher of Dorchester. Son of Mary, sister of John White. Freeman 1623. Constable 1628-29. On common council of freemen 1629-30. Lieutenant of militia 1642-43. Mayor 1649-50, 1661-62.

TOUPE, BERNARD (d. 1635). Of Dorchester. Probably son of Bartholomew of Devon and of Alice Gould. Thus related to diarist, who calls him "cousin". Married Margaret Pitt 1608. Burgess 1621. Bailiff 1628-29, 1629-30. Alderman 1630. Mayor 1634-35. Investor in Dorchester Company and in another New England venture.

TREGONNELL, JOHN (d. 1629?). Member of prosperous Dorset family of Milton Abbas. Great grandson of Sir John Tregonnell (d. 1565), an agent of Henry VIII in dissolution of monasteries. Married Katherine Browne, sister of Viscount Montague. Sheriff 1604, 1617. John (b. 1601) and Thomas were his sons.

TRENCHARD, SIR GEORGE (d. 1630). Of Wolfeton, near Dorchester. Influential in the county. Recorder of Dorchester by 1610 Charter. Of Puritan views. Removed, with Sir John Strangways, from his post of deputy lieutenant in 1625. Benefactor of Dorchester. Twice married, with one surviving son and six daughters, all of whom made useful marriage connections.

TRENCHARD, JOHN (b. 1596). Of Warmwell, which was given him by Sir George. Parliamentary partisan in Civil War. Member of Long Parliament and Dorset standing committee.

TRENCHARD, SIR THOMAS (1582-1657). Eldest son of Sir George. Sheriff 1634-35. Also parliamentarian and puritan.

TUTCHIE, ROBERT. Vicar of Fordington 1628; of Charminster 1634. Lecturer at Bridport 1642. Trier and lecturer at Chideock 1643. Rector of Bridport 1646.

UNDERWOOD, JOSEPH (b. 1586). Grocer of Dorchester. Constable 1625-26. Assistant to governor of freemen 1626-27, 1628-29, 1630-31, 1633-34. Overseer of poor for Trinity parish 1638.

UVEDALE, SIR WILLIAM. Of Horton, Dorset. Sheriff 1626. Notoriously covetous.

VAWTER, NICHOLAS. Burgess 1610. Benefactor of Dorchester.

WALKER, ROBERT. Married to diarist's sister-in-law, Margaret Parkins, by John White 1623. Godfather to diarist's son John 1625.

WALTHAM, HENRY (b. 1581). Merchant and magistrate of Weymouth-Melcombe Regis, like his brother Thomas (b. 1594). A ship owner, he engaged in the Newfoundland trade. Owned two privateers 1630. Possibly related to diarist.

WATT, JOHN (d. 1627). Factor in New England for the Dorchester Company. Brother-in-law of Richard Bushrode.

WAY, GEORGE (d. 1641). Glover of Dorchester. Governor of hospital 1626. Constable 1625-26, 1634-35. Churchwarden 1629. Investor in Dorchester Company and other New England ventures.

WHETCOMBE, JOHN (1580-1635). Rector of Maiden Newton 1610-35, and of Frome Vauchurch 1620-35.

WHITE, JOHN (1575-1648). Called Patriarch of Dorchester. Appointed rector of Holy Trinity, Dorchester, 1606. A Puritan exercising much influence over borough. From 1624 involved in formation of Massachusetts Company, a project to send a colony of men there, which sailed 1629. Took covenant 1640. Fled to Savoy 1642 after house plundered. Ministered at Lambeth from 1643. Buried at St Peter's.
(See F. Rose-Troup, *John White, The Patriarch of Dorchester*)

WHITEFIELD, SAMUEL (1600-28). Rector of All Saints, Dorchester, 1627-28.

WHITEWAY, JOHN (1614-79). Brother of diarist, twin brother of Samuel. Substantial merchant and influential magistrate of Dorchester. Married, as his first wife, Mary White, niece of John White. Early an office holder. Capital burgess 1641. Bailiff 1642, 1650, 1651, 1660. Mayor 1646, 1658. MP for Dorchester 1654, 1656, 1660. Captain of one of the companies defending Dorchester 1643, and among those surrendering the town to the Royalists. After Restoration disconnected himself from Dorchester, acquiring property in Rickmansworth, Hertfordshire, where he died.

WHITEWAY, MARY (b. 1615). Sister of diarist. Moved to London 1631, probably on her marriage to Andrew Kenricke (or Kerry).

WHITEWAY, SAMUEL (b. 1614). Brother of diarist, twin brother of John. Matriculated St Catherine's College, Cambridge, 1631. BA 1635., Died before 1640.

[183]

WHITEWAY, WILLIAM (1570-1640). Father of diarist. Merchant of Dorchester. Successful in trade, especially with France. Born at Denbury, Devon, he left home town to follow fortunes as apprentice merchant. First visited Dorchester 1585. Imprisoned as a Protestant in Honfleur, France, 1590. Married Mary Mounsell, herself from a trading family, 1598. Settled permanently in Dorchester 1600, and soon an office-holder. Listed as capital burgess in 1610 Charter, and as alderman in 1629 Charter. Four times bailiff, including 1626 and 1635. Mayor 1631. MP for Dorchester 1624, 1625. He and his wife outlived most of their children.

WHITEWAY, WILLIAM (1599-1635). The diarist. Merchant of Dorchester, where he attended the free school under Robert Cheeke. First journey to France 1616. Married to Elinor Parkins in Holy Trinity by John White 1620. Freeman 1621. Lieutenant in militia 1622. Assistant to governor of freemen 1622. Governor 1624. Capital burgess 1624. MP for Dorchester 1626. Steward of hospital 1626. Overseer of poor for Holy Trinity parish 1628. Bailiff 1629, 1633. Town steward 1630. Feoffee of All Saints church 1633. See family tree for his children. His "Private Chronology" is printed in *Proceedings of the Dorset Natural History and Antiquarian Field Club*, Vol. XVI, pp. 59-75.

WHITEWAY, WILLIAM (1622-?1656). Son of the diarist. Apart from the posthumous daughter Mary, William was the only one of his children who outlived the diarist.

WILLIAMS, JOHN (d. 1632). Member of ancient Dorset family of Herringston, south of Dorchester. Married Jane, daughter of Sir George Trenchard, 1613. Keeper of royal manor of Fordington. Captain of Dorset horse 1628.

YEATE, GEORGE. Fishmonger of Dorchester. Freeman 1621.

YEATE, JOHN. Clothier of Dorchester. Capital burgess 1610.

INDEX OF PERSONAL NAMES
IN THE DIARY

Righton, Lawrence, 151
Rives, Richard, 155, Mr., 97
Rivet, Dr., 144
Roberts, John, 113, Mr., 133
Robins, Alderman, 151
Rochfoucault, Earl of, 44
Rogers, Mr., 57
Rohan, M. de, 45
Rolles, Mr., 135, 151, 153
Roxburgh, Countess of, 119
Roy, Agnes, 155, Mr., 65
Rulizius, John, 93, 120, 123, 149, 158
Russell, Mr., 129
Rutland, Earl of, 50, 53, 126
Ryves, Sir John, 67

Sacheverell, Mr., 122
Sadleir, Sir Thomas, 155
St George, Sir Henry, 53
St John, Sir John, 58
Salleneuve, Captain, 127, 133
Saltonstall, Sir Richard, 140
Sambourne, Richard, 24, 111
Sandford, Tobiah, 53, Mrs., 110
Sands, Sir Edwin, 38
Sarsfield, Viscount, 136
Savage, Elisabeth, 155, Richard, 27, 48, 54, 65, 92, 99, 113, 130, 151, William, 87, 118, Mrs., 107
Savoy, Charles Emmanuel I, Duke of, 24
Saxony, John George, Elector of, 30, 119
Schloer, Frederick, 121
Searchfield, Dr., 49
Seimer, Sir Francis, 77
Selden, Mr., 38, 81
Seward, John, 153
Seymour, Sir Francis, 80
Sheffield, Lord, 76
Sheldon, Sir Richard, 118, Mr., 133
Shelton, Mr., 76
Shepherd, William, 50, Mr., 34
Sherfield, Mr., 142
Sherland, Mr., 81

Shervill, Mr., 128
Shrewsbury, Earl of, 110
Sibthorpe, Dr., 91
Sigismund III, King of Poland, 40, 124
Simmes, Anne, 124
Simons, Mr., 133
Simpson, Captain, 117
Sims, Henry, 65, 118, William, 131
Skimmerton, Captain, 116
Skypwith, Mr., 116
Sleer, Mr., 88
Small, John, 114
Smart, Robert, 133, 136
Smith, George, 162, Sir Thomas, 26, 76
Smitheyes, Sir Arthur, 60, 61
Soissons, Louis, Count of, 68
Somerset, Earl of, 38, 43, 50, 107, Countess of, 124
Soubise, Benjamin, Count of, 45–48, 68, 75, 90, 135
South, Mr., 142
Southampton, Earl of, 38, 62, 66
Spalata, Archbishop of, 68
Sparrow, Thomas, 100, 103, 113
Speed, John, 4
Speering, Mr. 44
Spencer, Lord, 36, 37
Spicer, John, 56, Mrs., 129
Spinola, Ambrogio, Marquis of las Balbasas, 31, 35, 41, 47, 49, 60, 64, 66, 71, 72, 73, 75, 77
Spratlin, Andrew, 142
Spry, Sir Henry, 94
Stanford, Captain, 105
Stephens, John, 115, 118, 155, Roger, 120
Still, Thomas, 99, 106
Stone, Nicholas, 134
Stowell, Sir John, 151
Strangways, Sir John, 32, 57, 71, 72, 79, 83, 87, 89, 94, 95, 100, 131, 142, 148, 154
Strickland, John, 123, 127, 132
Strode, Sir John, 32, 71, Sir Richard,